"It's classic burlesque. Probably the most infuriating thing of all for her bullies is that she looks like she's having a really good time."

— Emma Lewis,
Assistant Curator, Tate Modern, London

The
Bully
Pulpit

Haley
Morris-
Cafiero

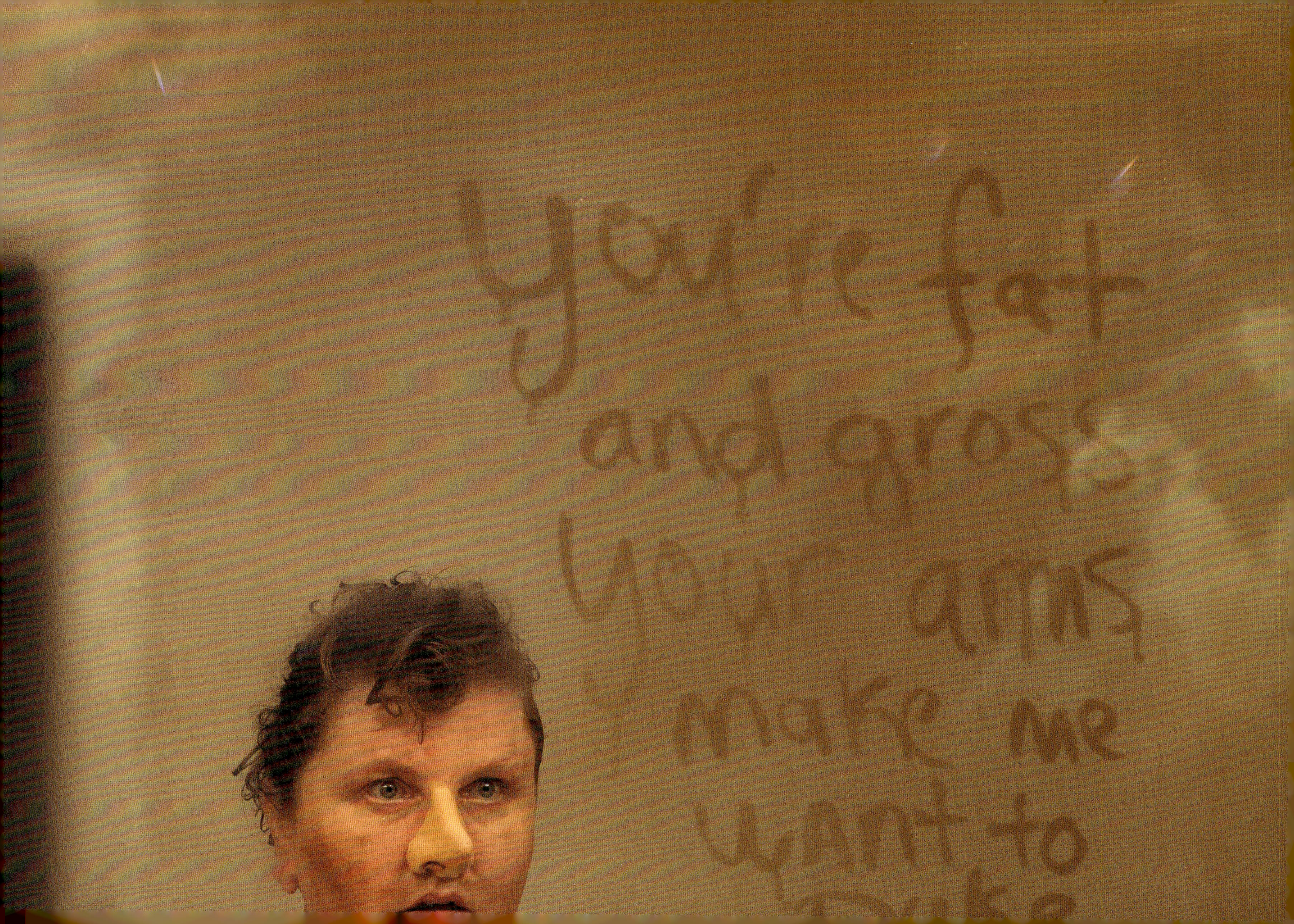

You're fat
and gross
your arms
make me
want to

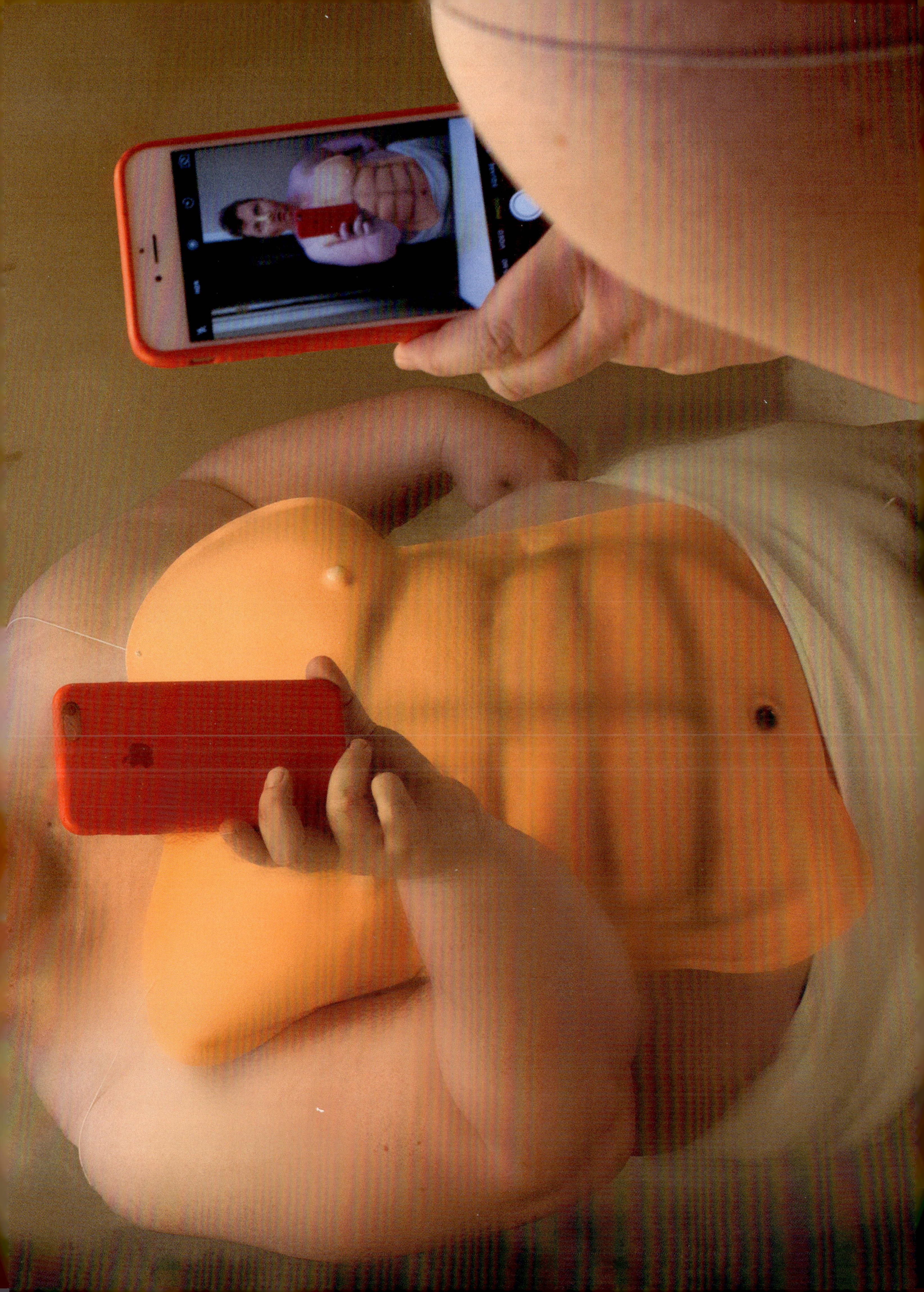

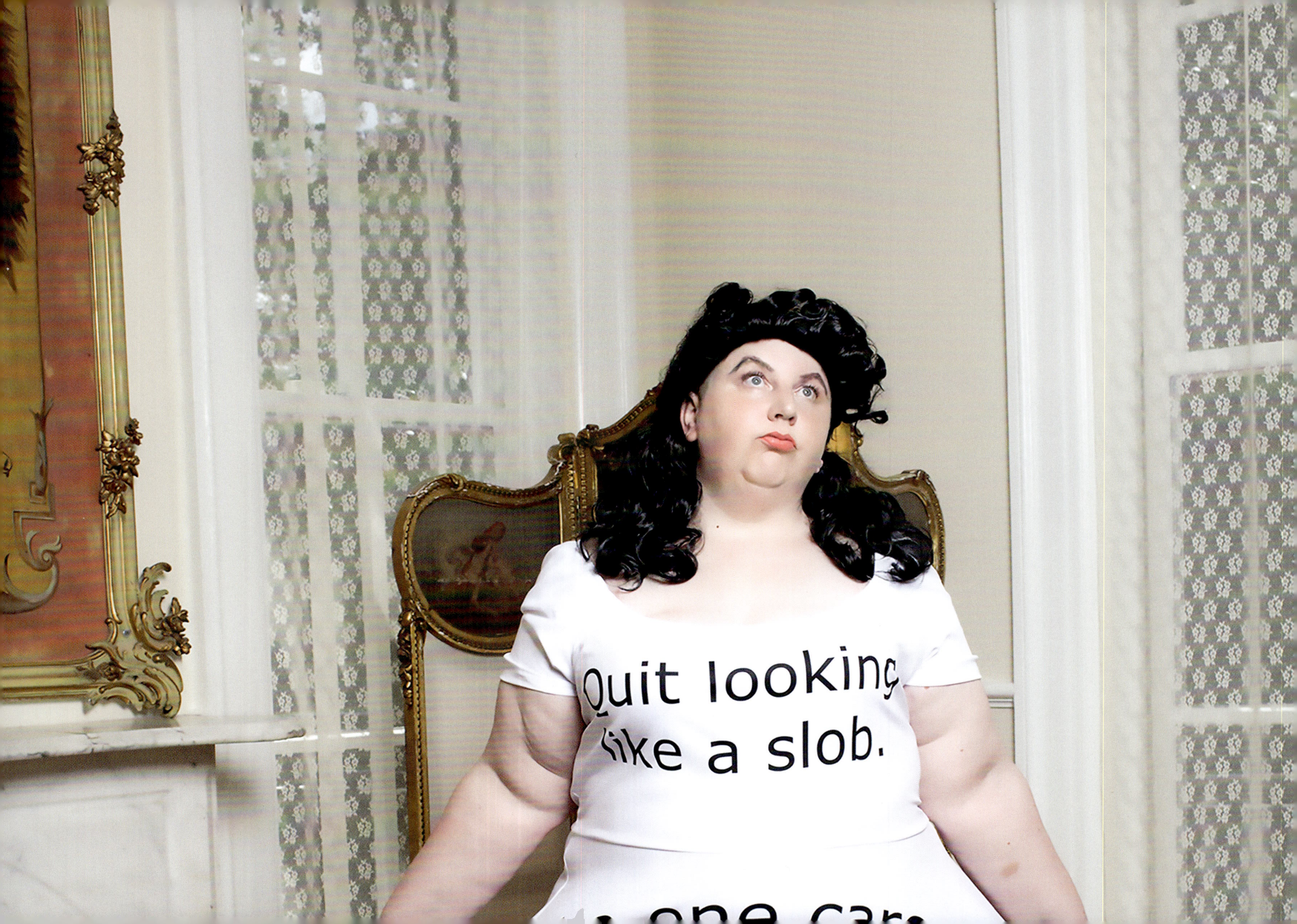
Quit looking
like a slob.
one car

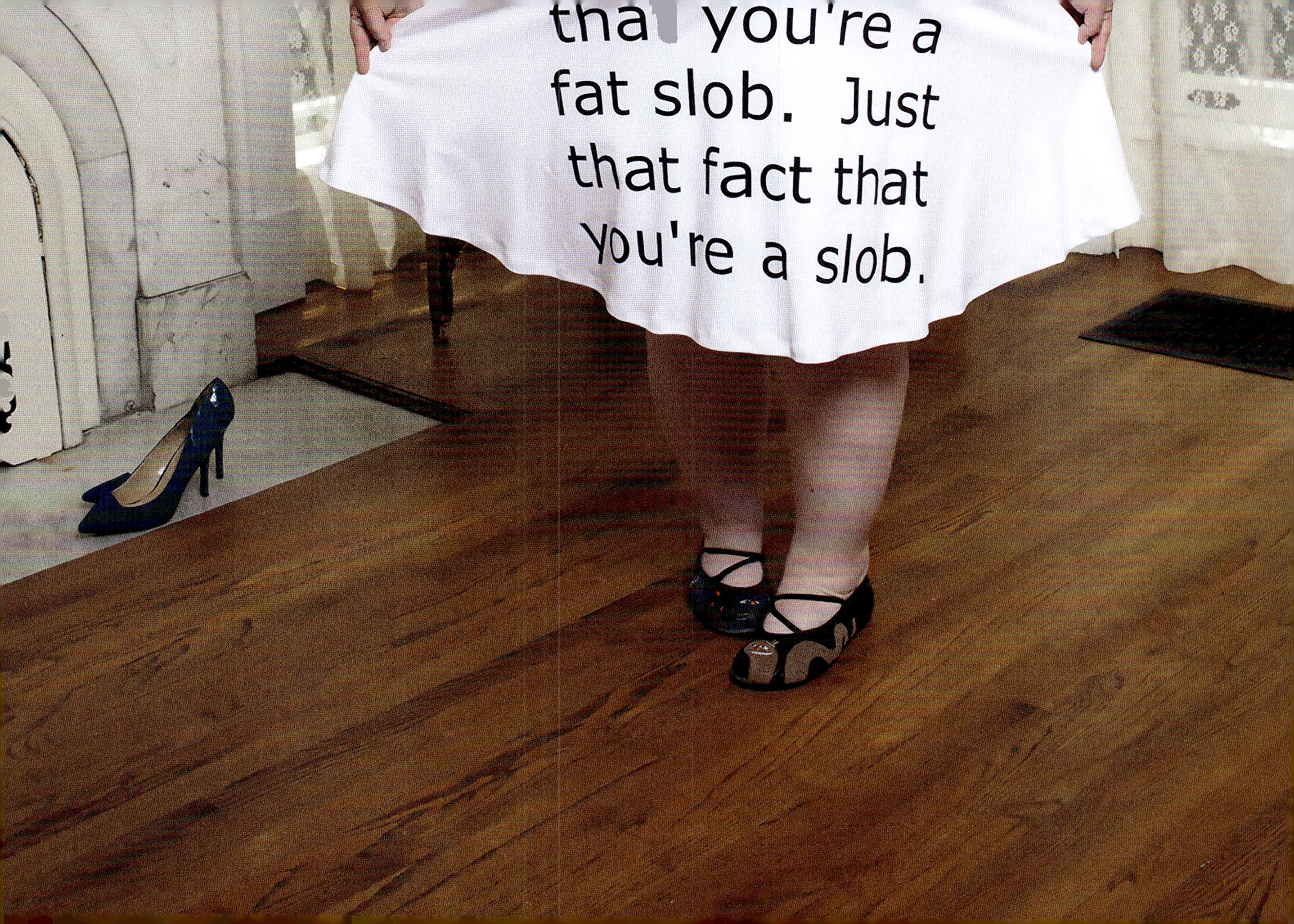

that you're a
fat slob. Just
that fact that
you're a slob.

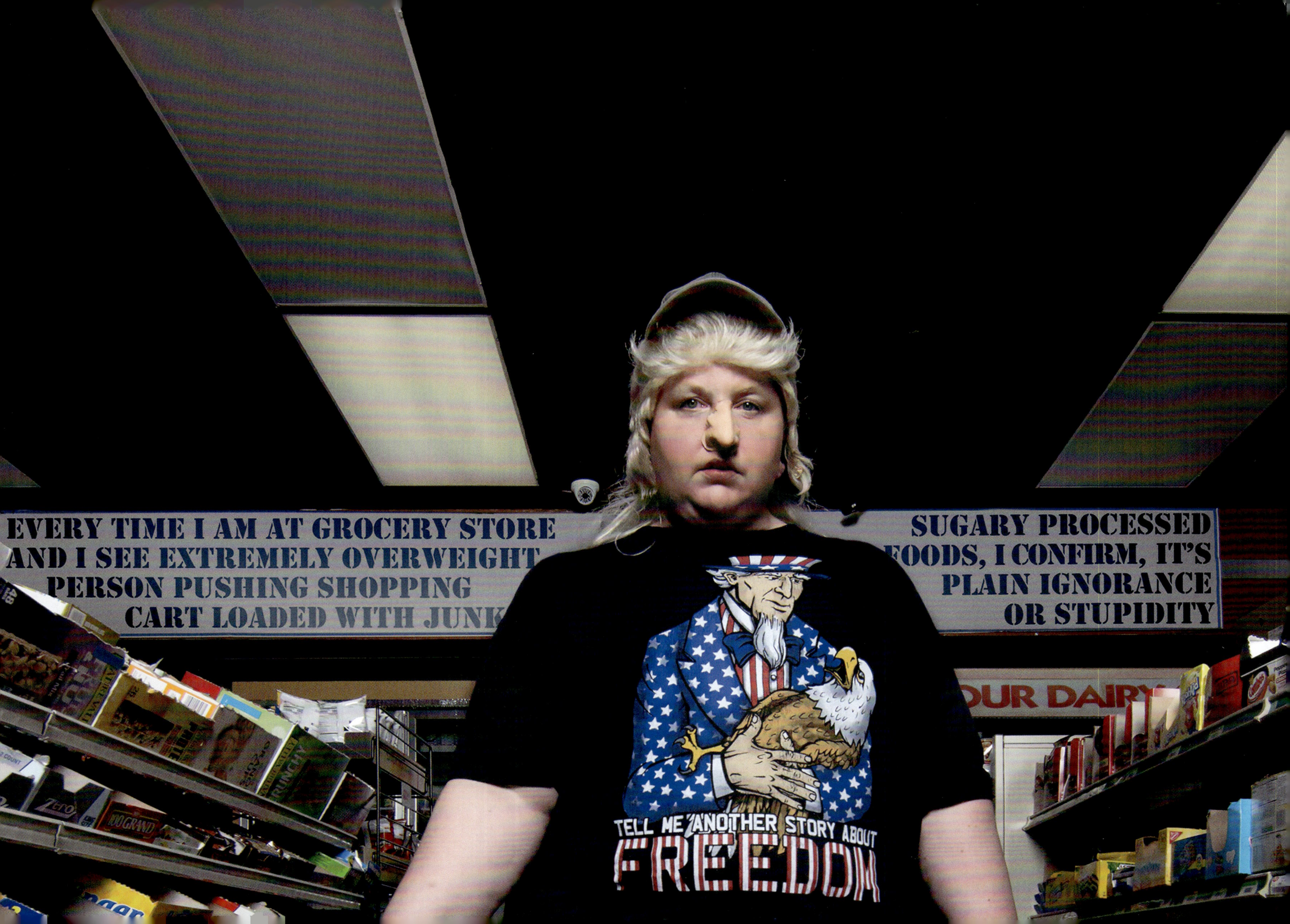

EVERY TIME I AM AT GROCERY STORE AND I SEE EXTREMELY OVERWEIGHT PERSON PUSHING SHOPPING CART LOADED WITH JUNK
SUGARY PROCESSED FOODS, I CONFIRM, IT'S PLAIN IGNORANCE OR STUPIDITY
TELL ME ANOTHER STORY ABOUT FREEDOM
OUR DAIRY

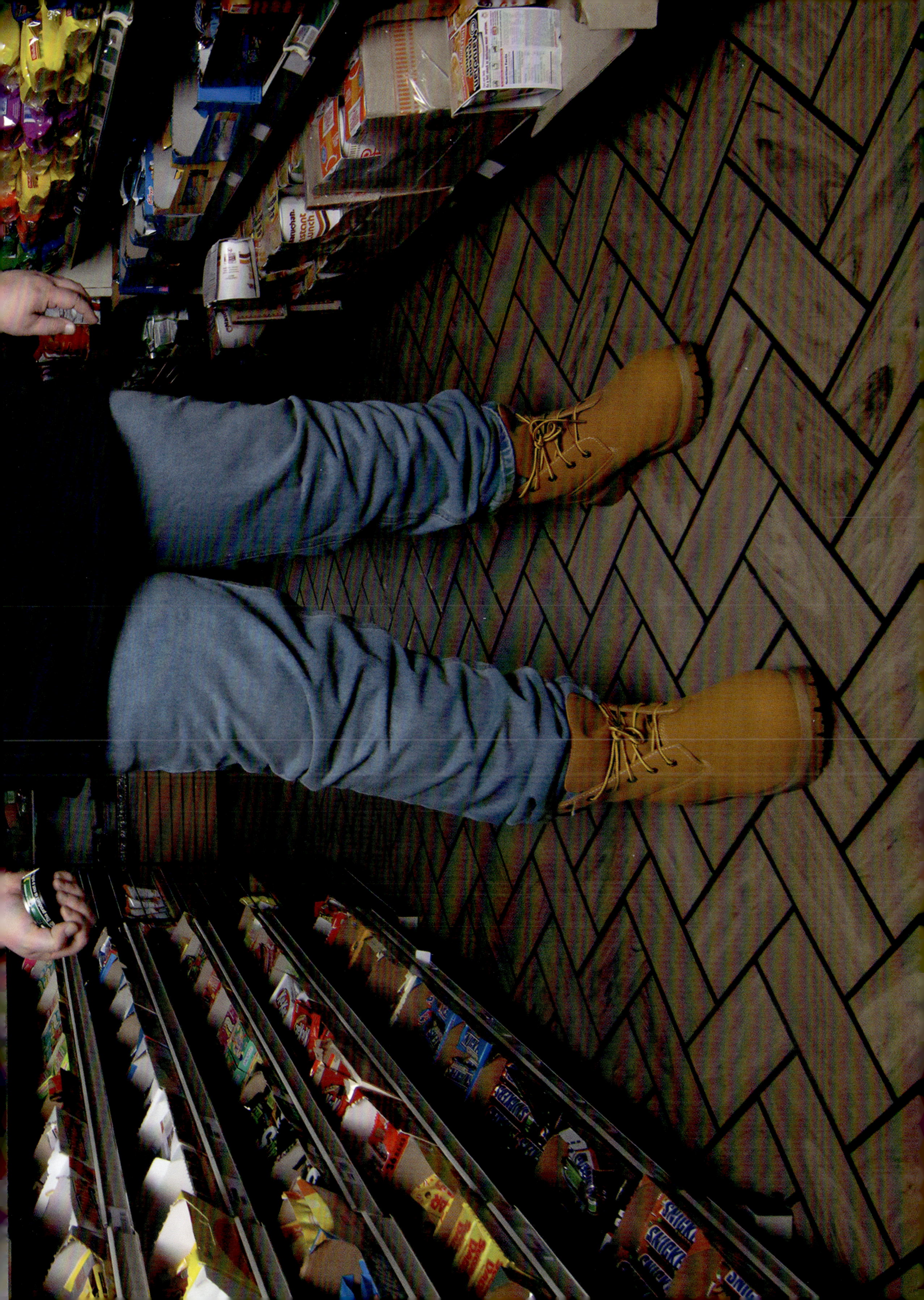

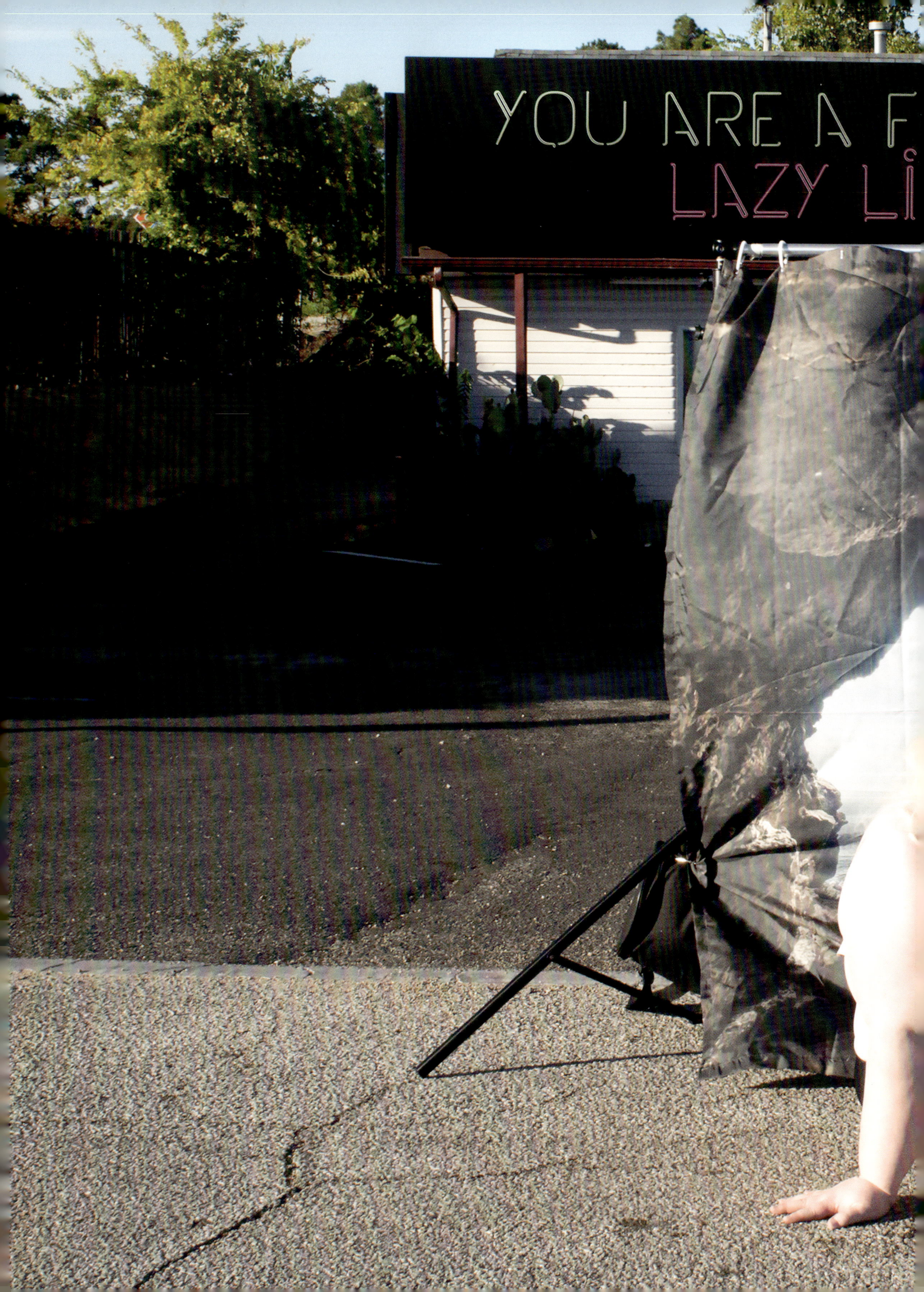
YOU ARE A F
LAZY LI

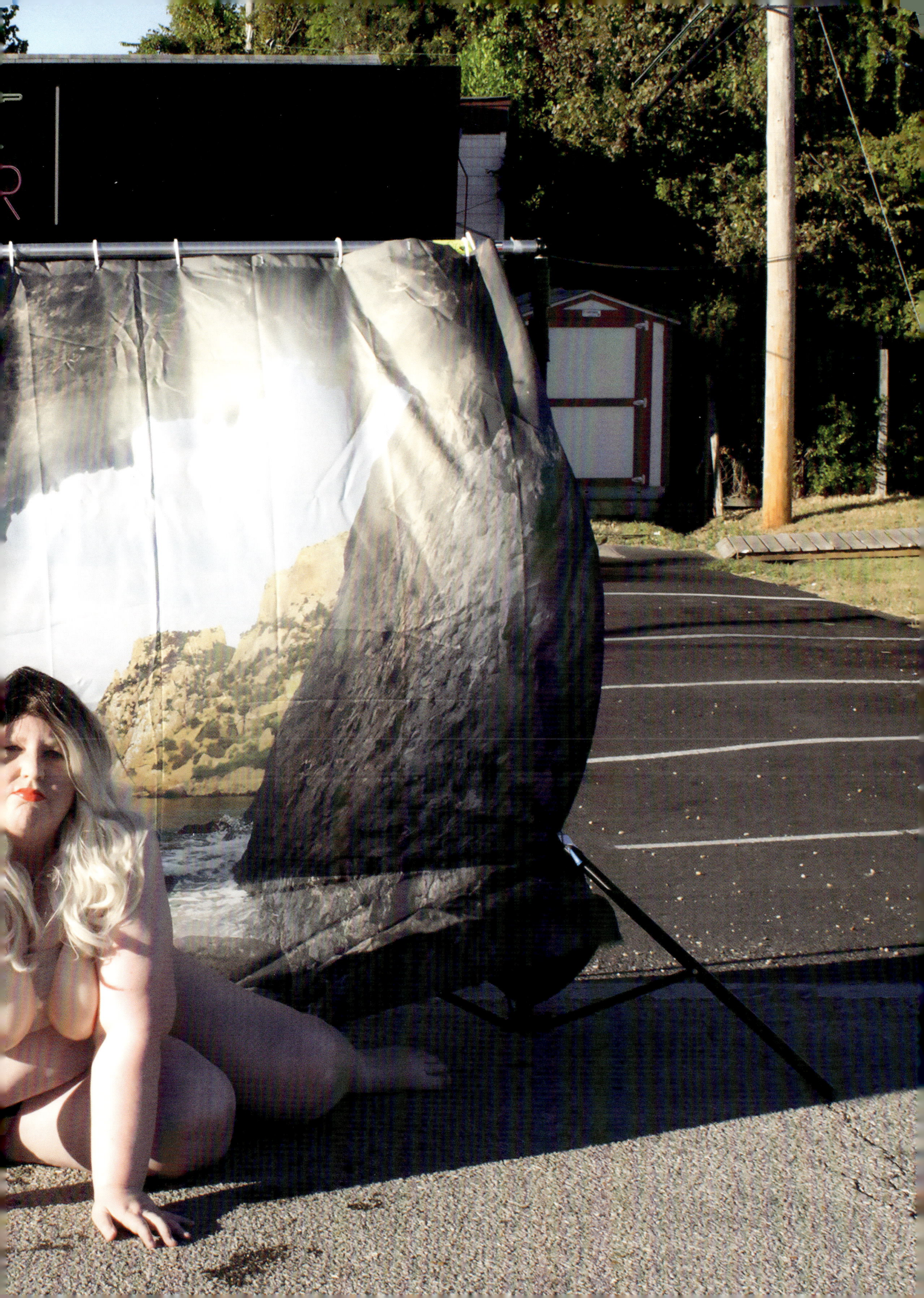

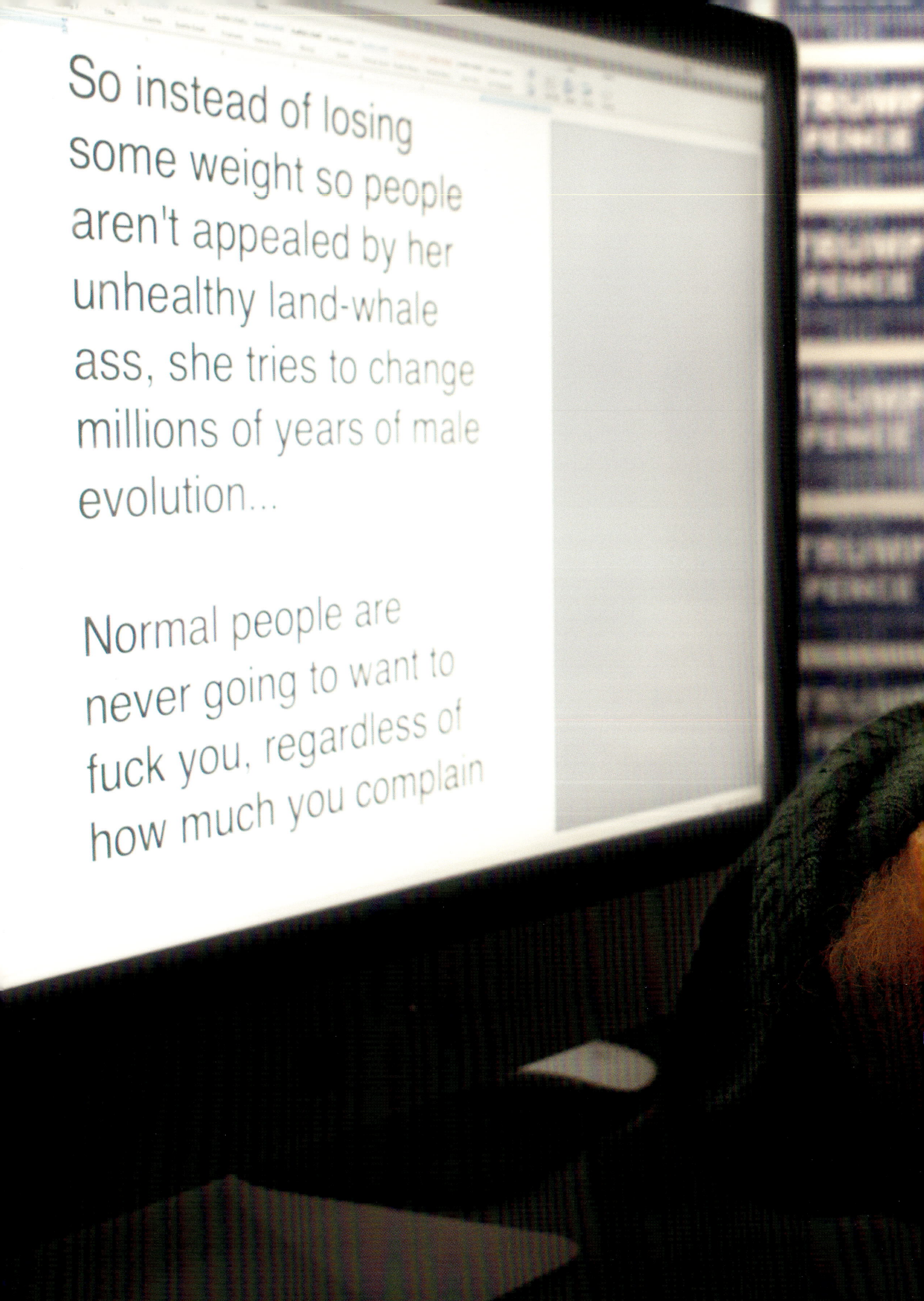
So instead of losing some weight so people aren't appealed by her unhealthy land-whale ass, she tries to change millions of years of male evolution...

Normal people are never going to want to fuck you, regardless of how much you complain

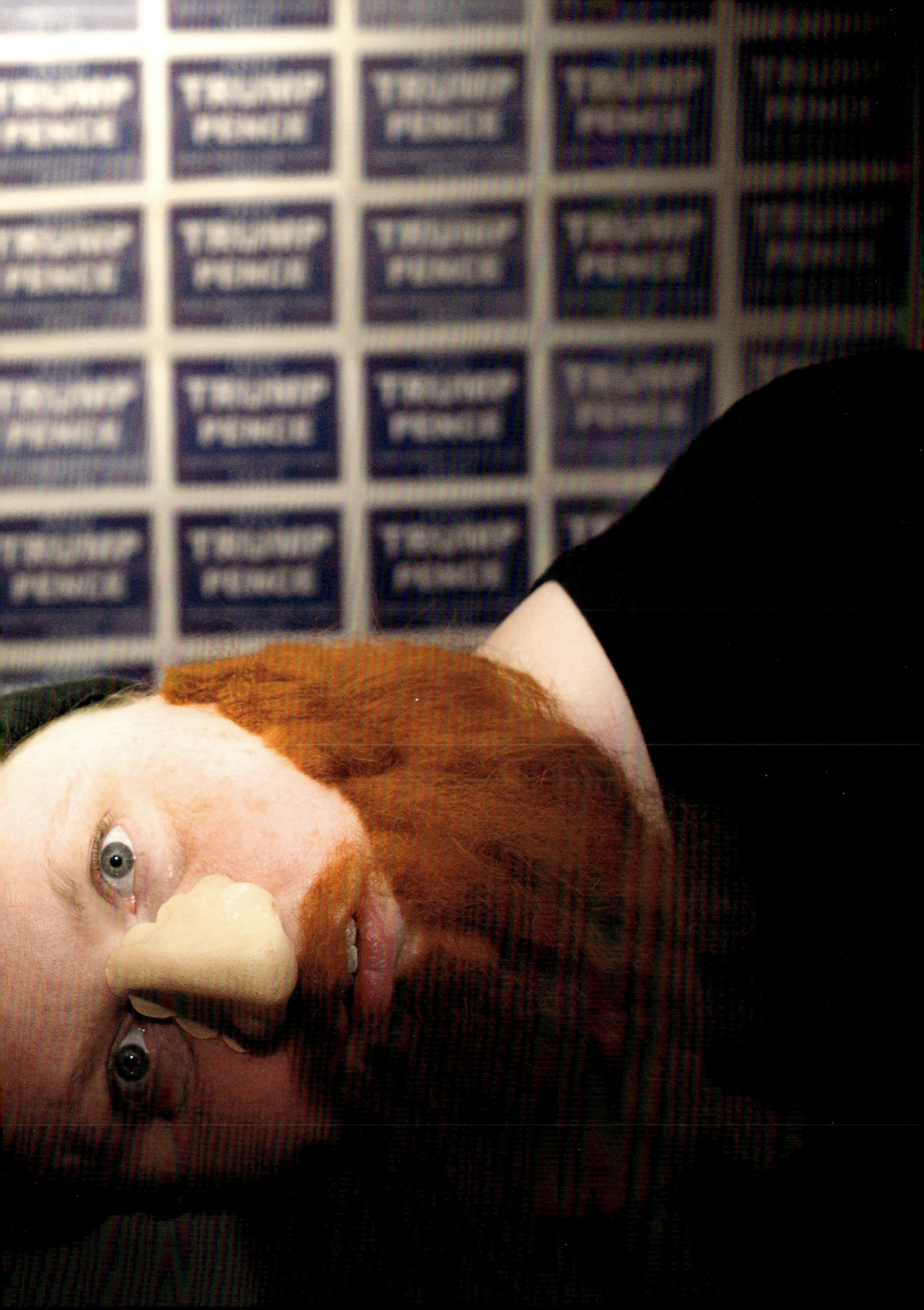

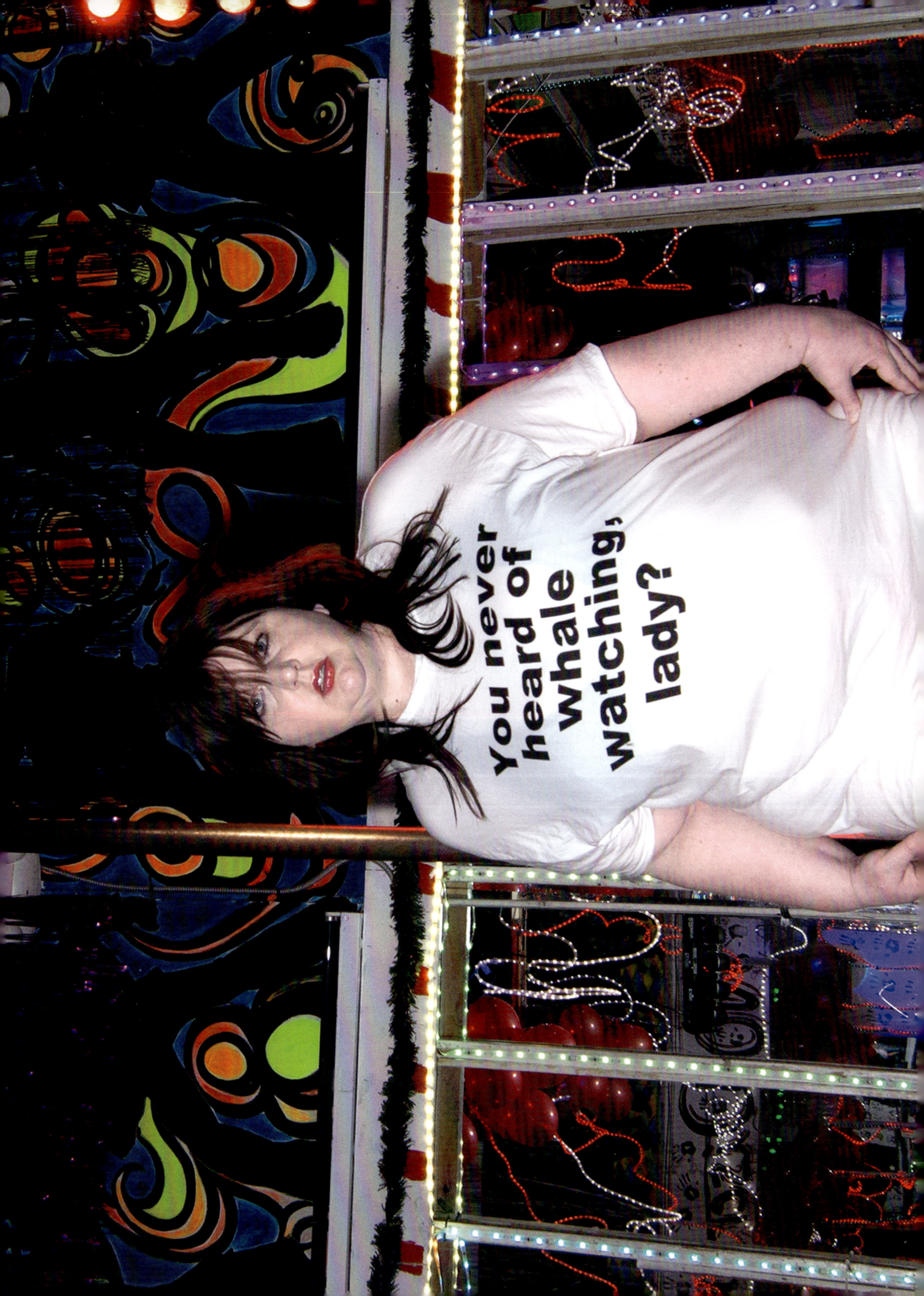
You never heard of whale watching, lady?

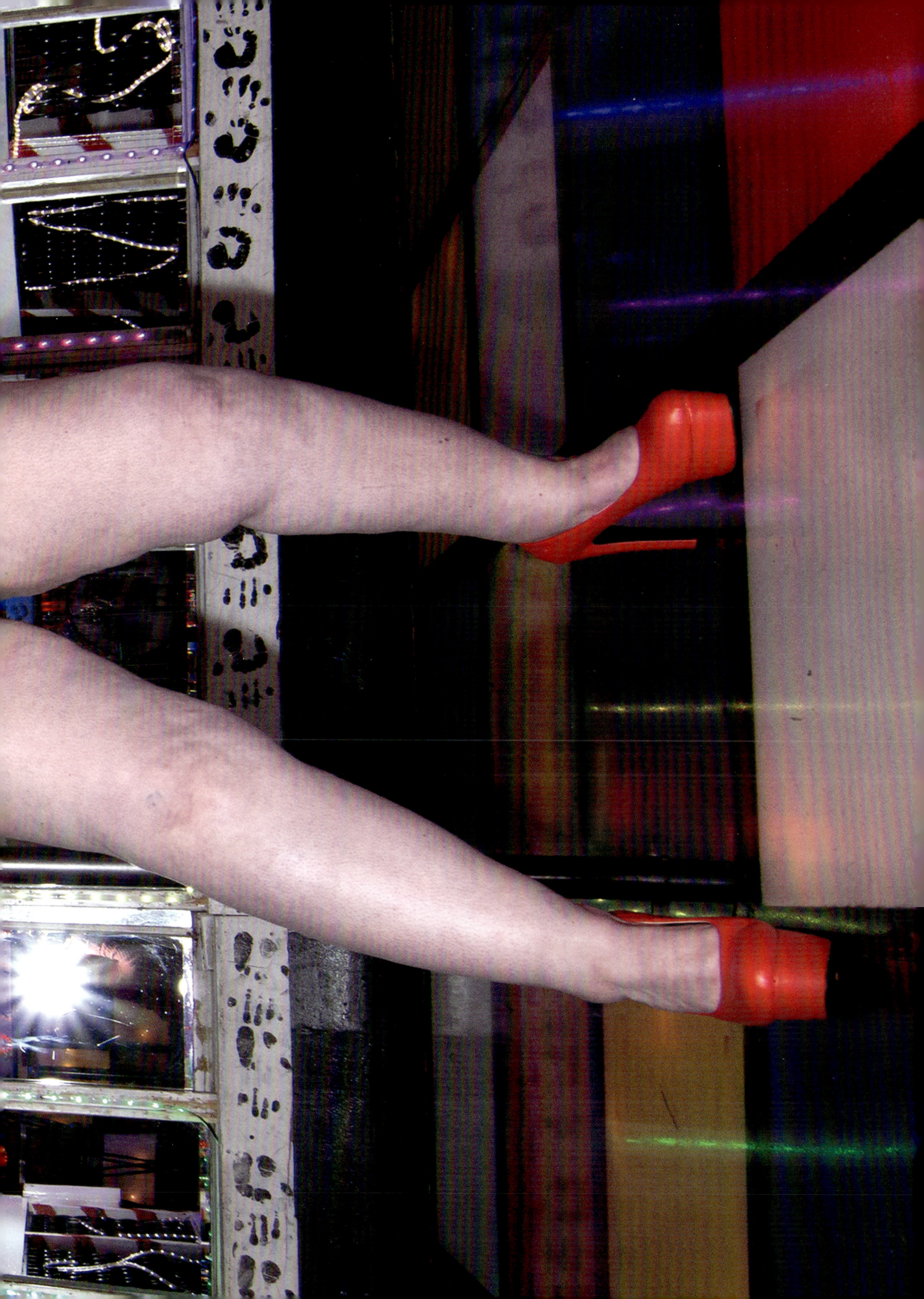

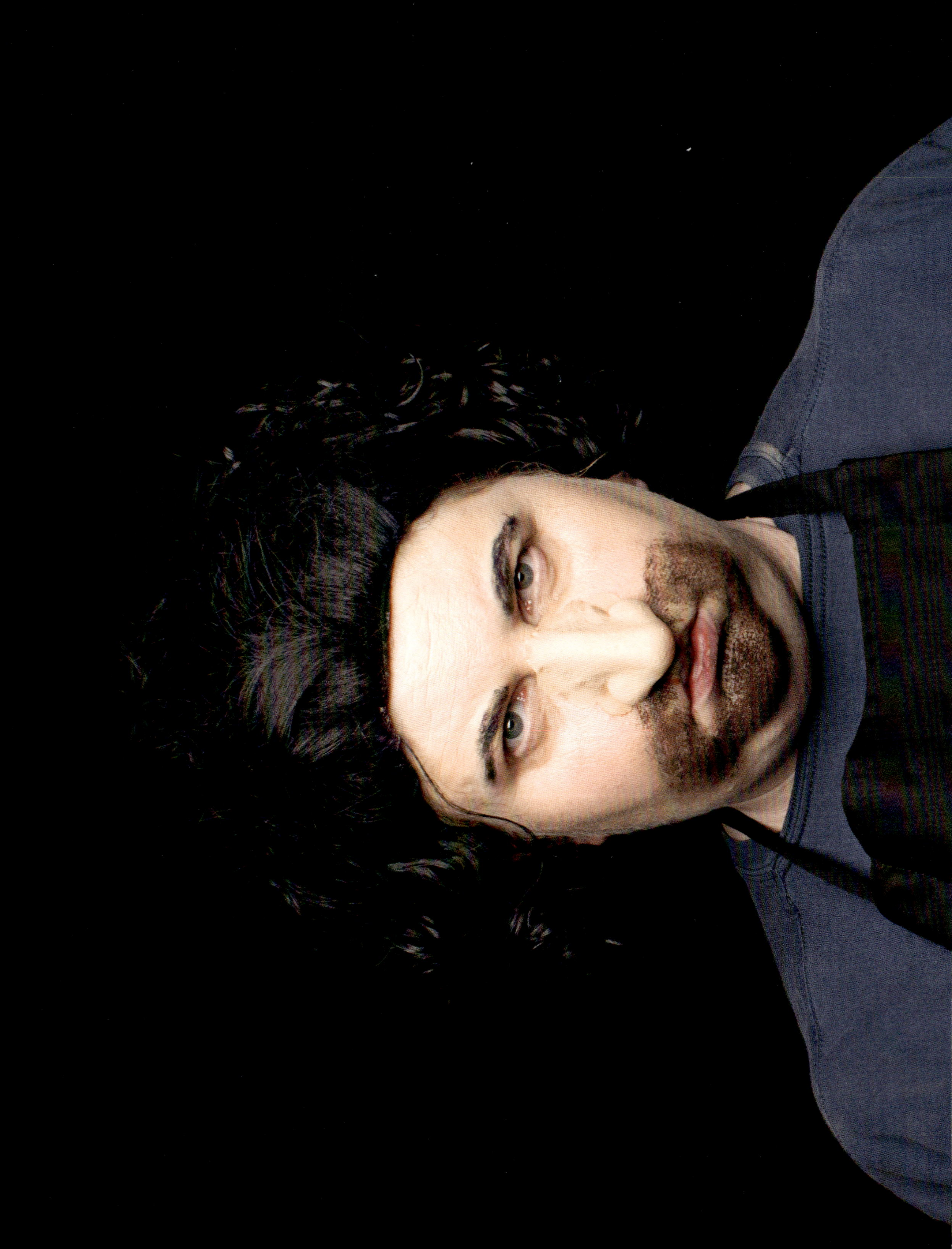

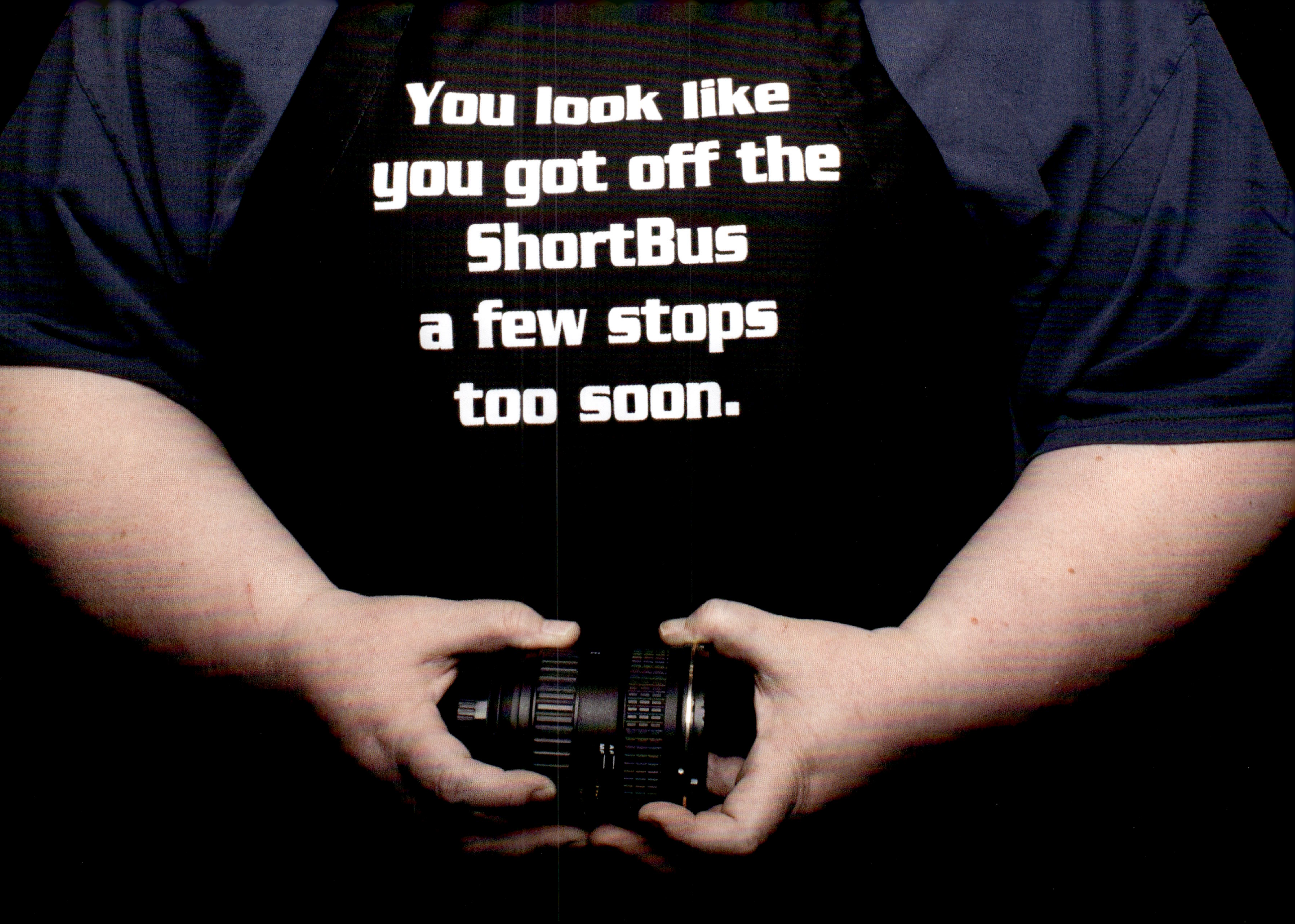
You look like
you got off the
ShortBus
a few stops
too soon.

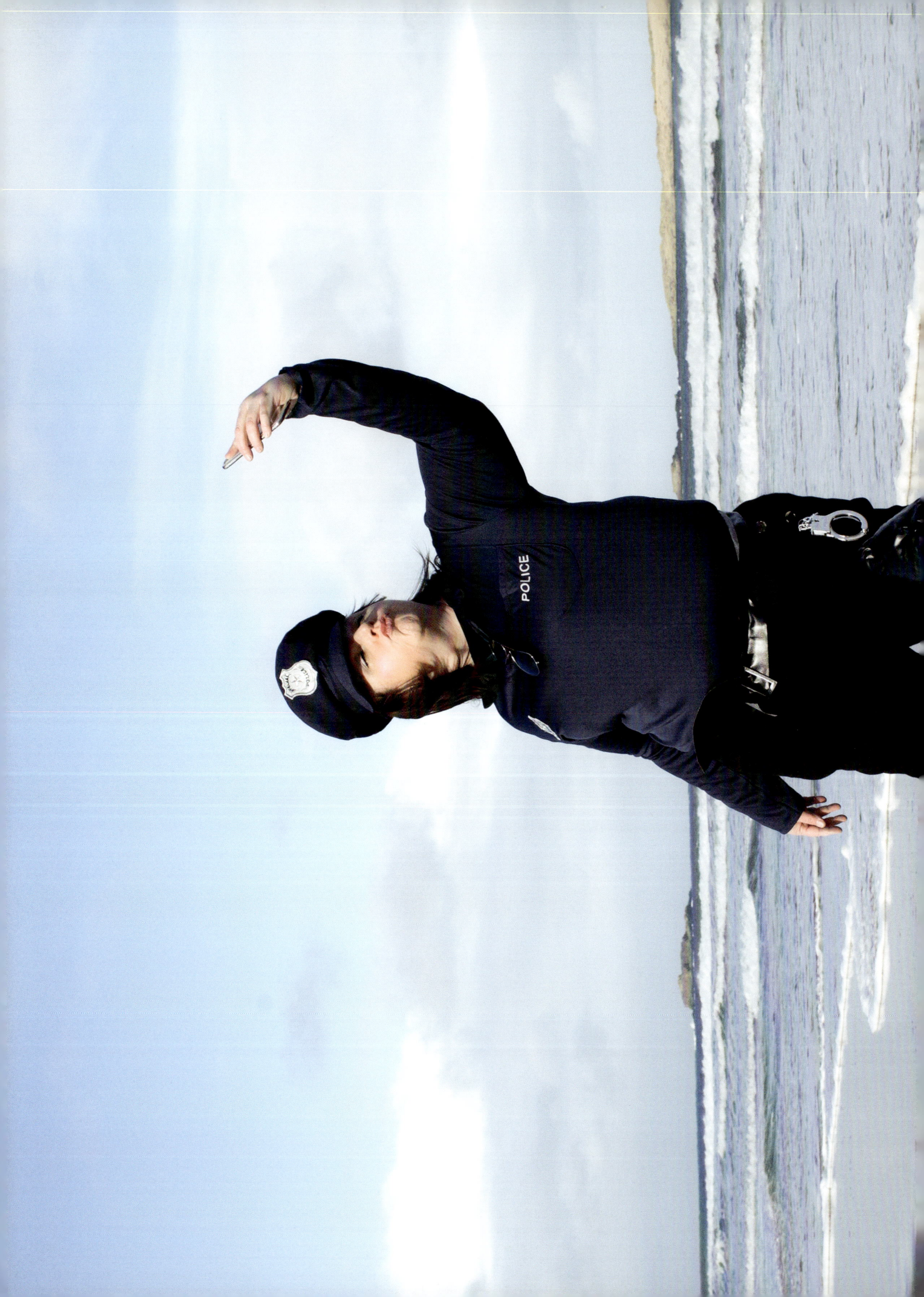

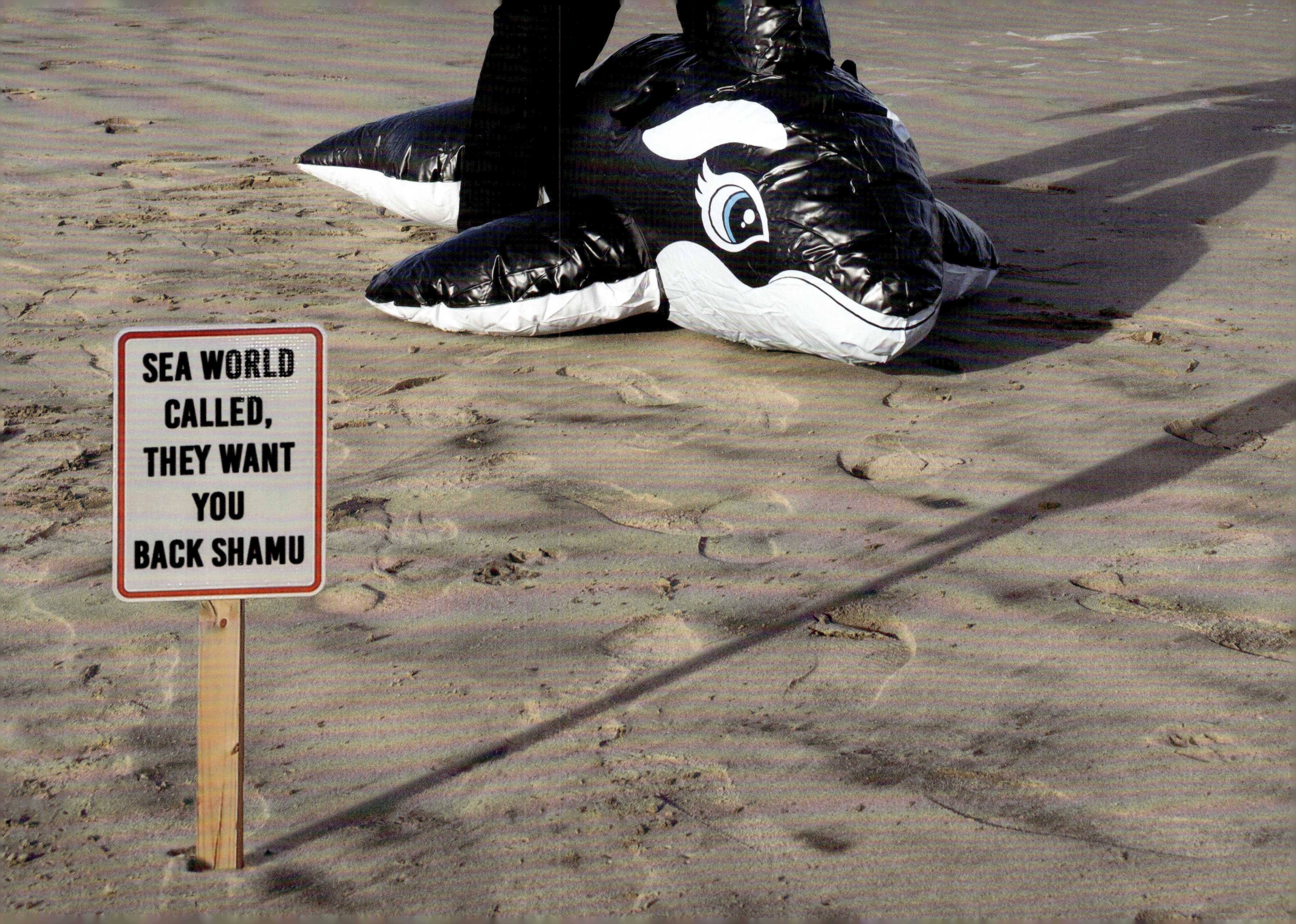

SEA WORLD
CALLED,
THEY WANT
YOU
BACK SHAMU

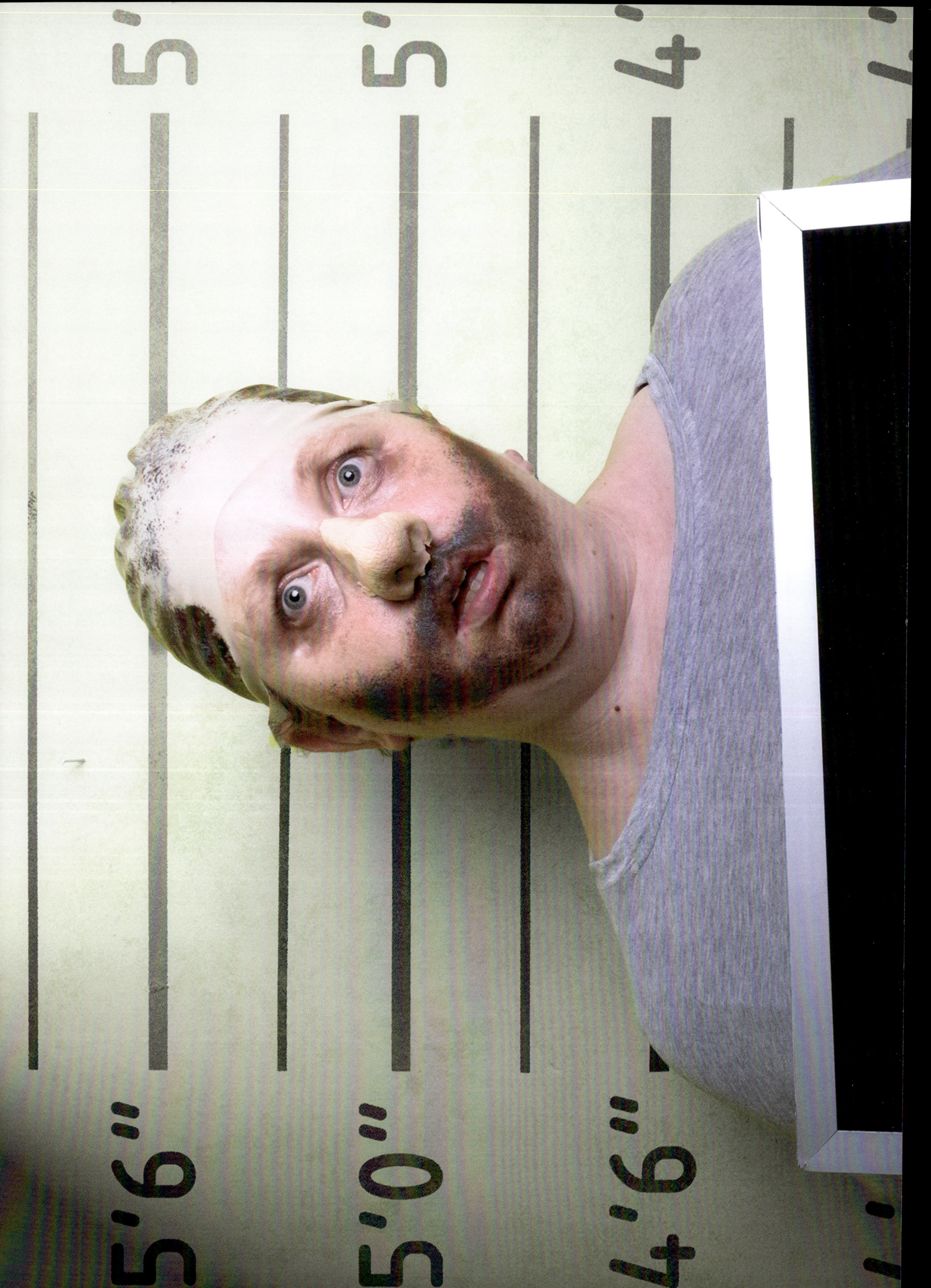

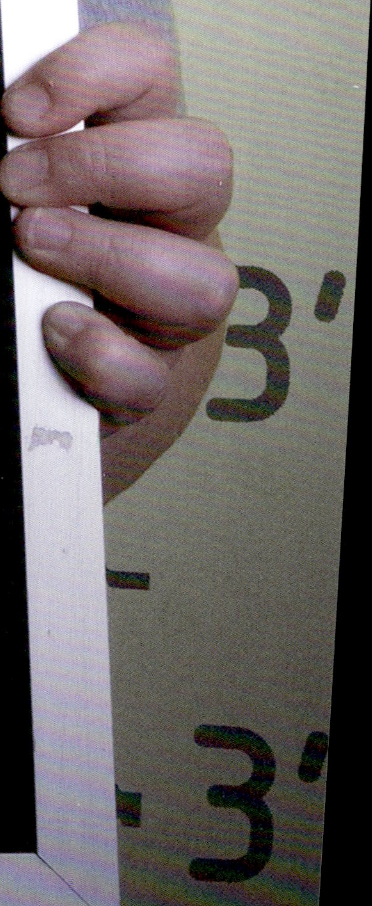

YOUR *WORK* OPENS
YOU UP TO
CRITICISM

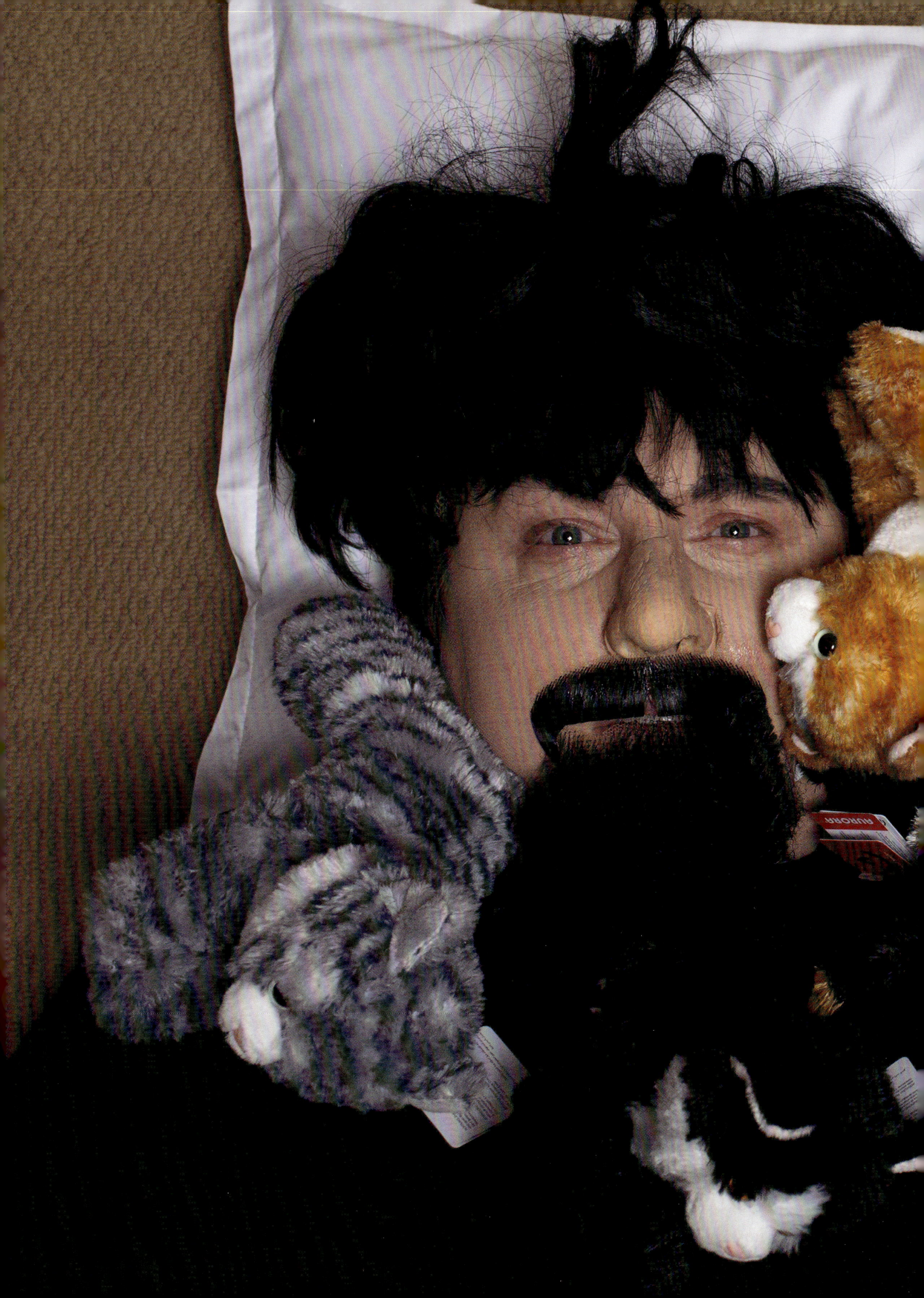

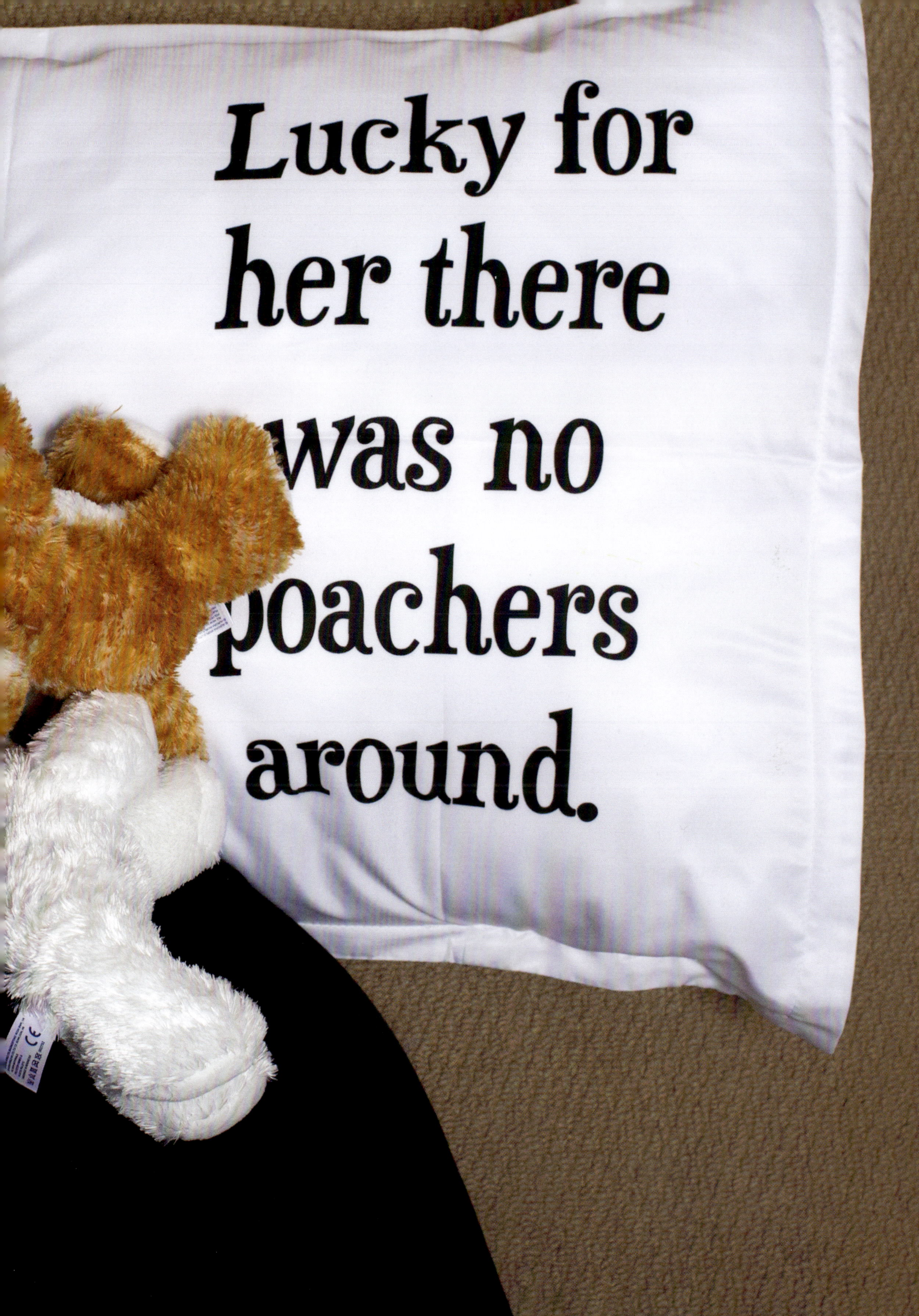

Lucky for her there was no poachers around.

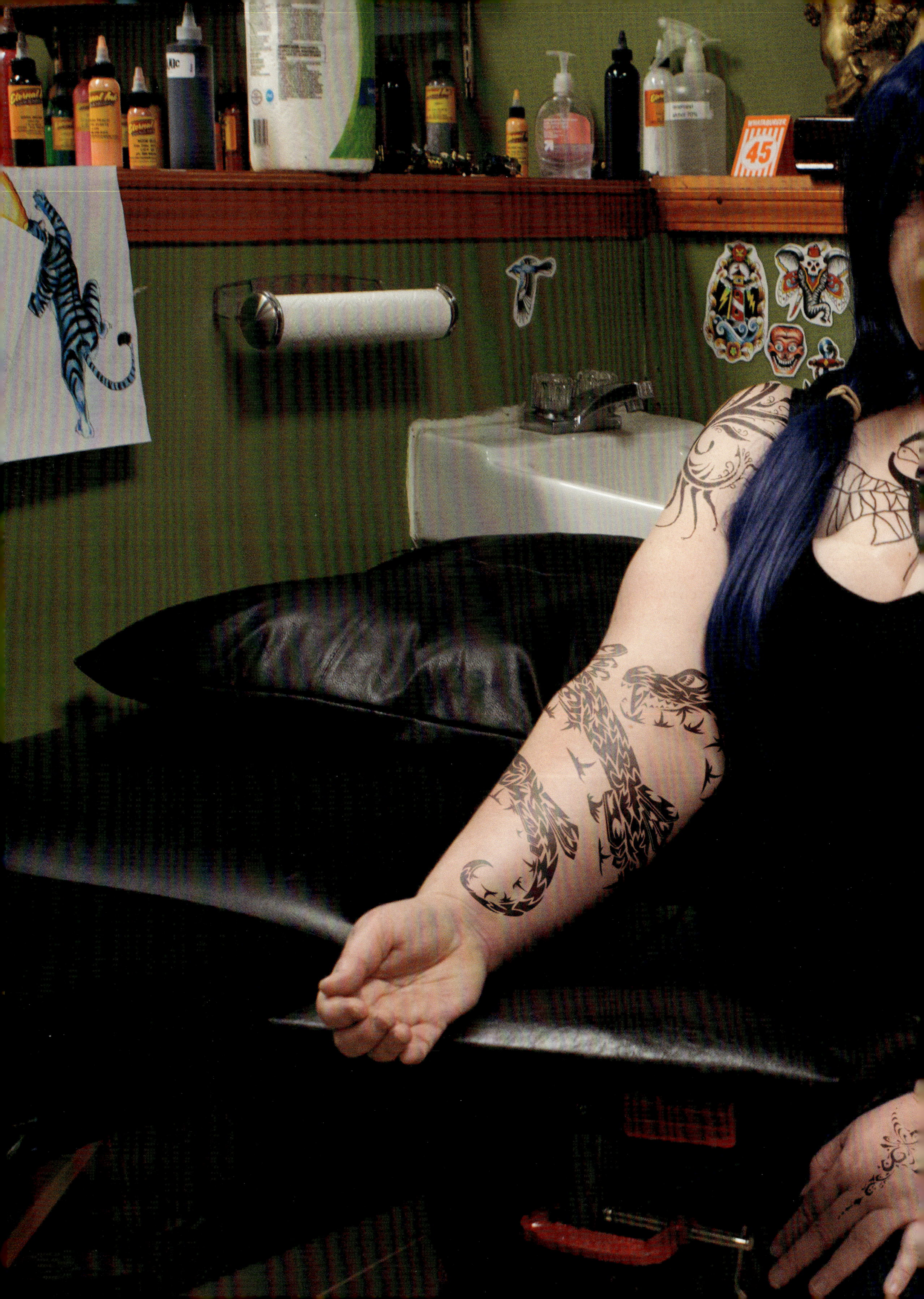

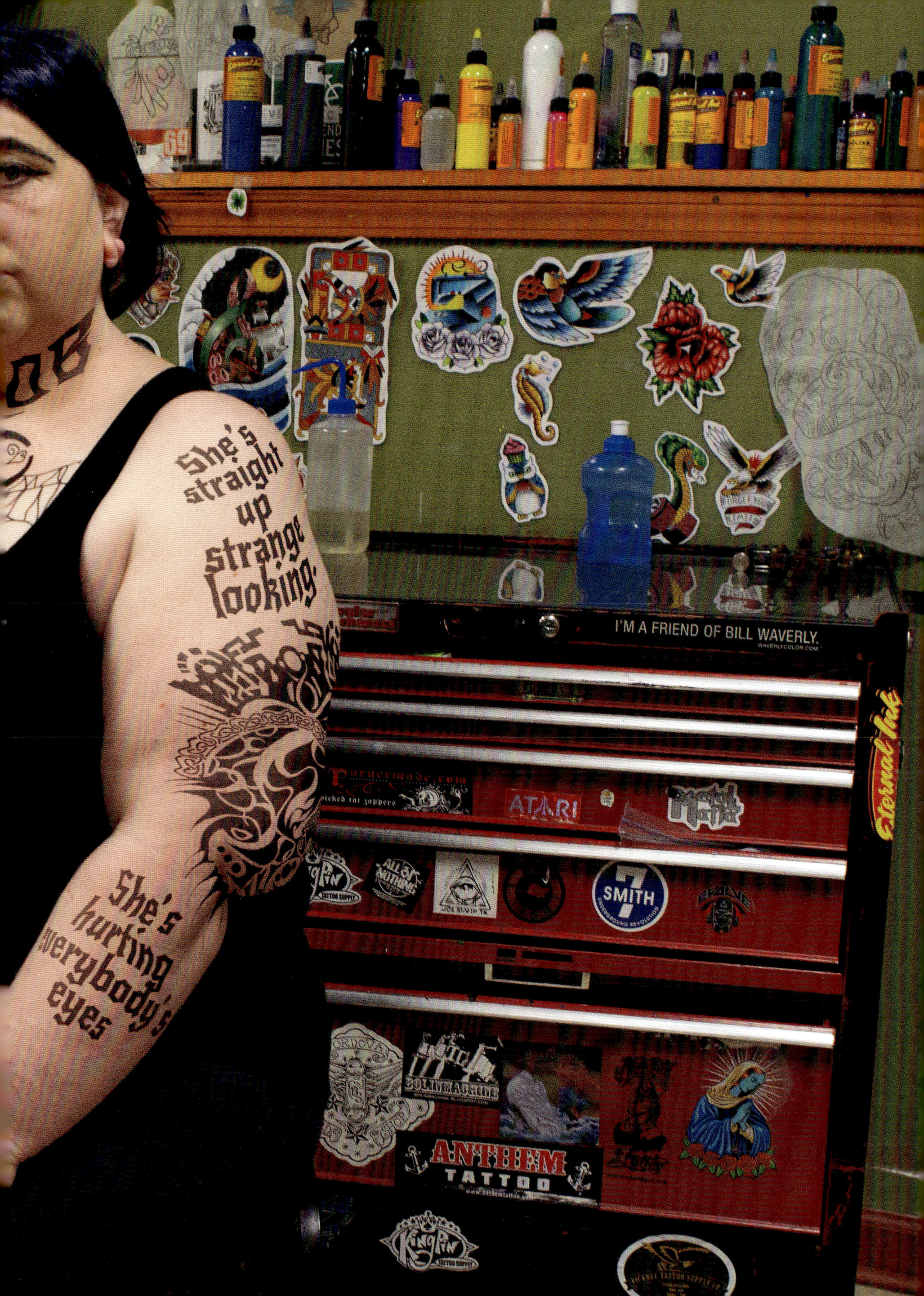

She's straight up strange looking.
She's hurting everybody's eyes
I'M A FRIEND OF BILL WAVERLY.
WAVERLYCOLOR.COM
Eternal Ink
ATARI
SMITH
7
ANTHEM TATTOO
KingPin

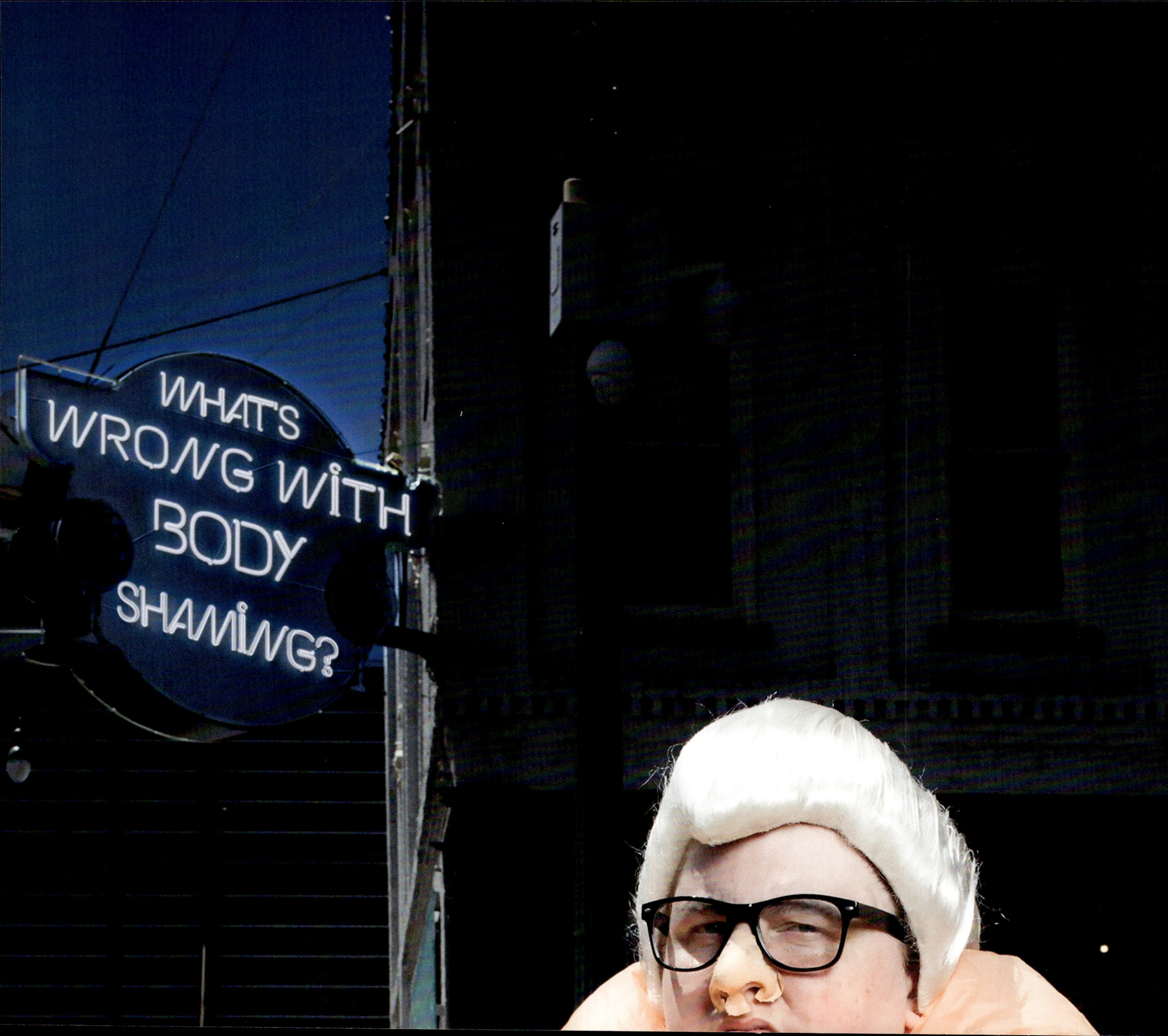

WHAT'S
WRONG WITH
BODY
SHAMING?

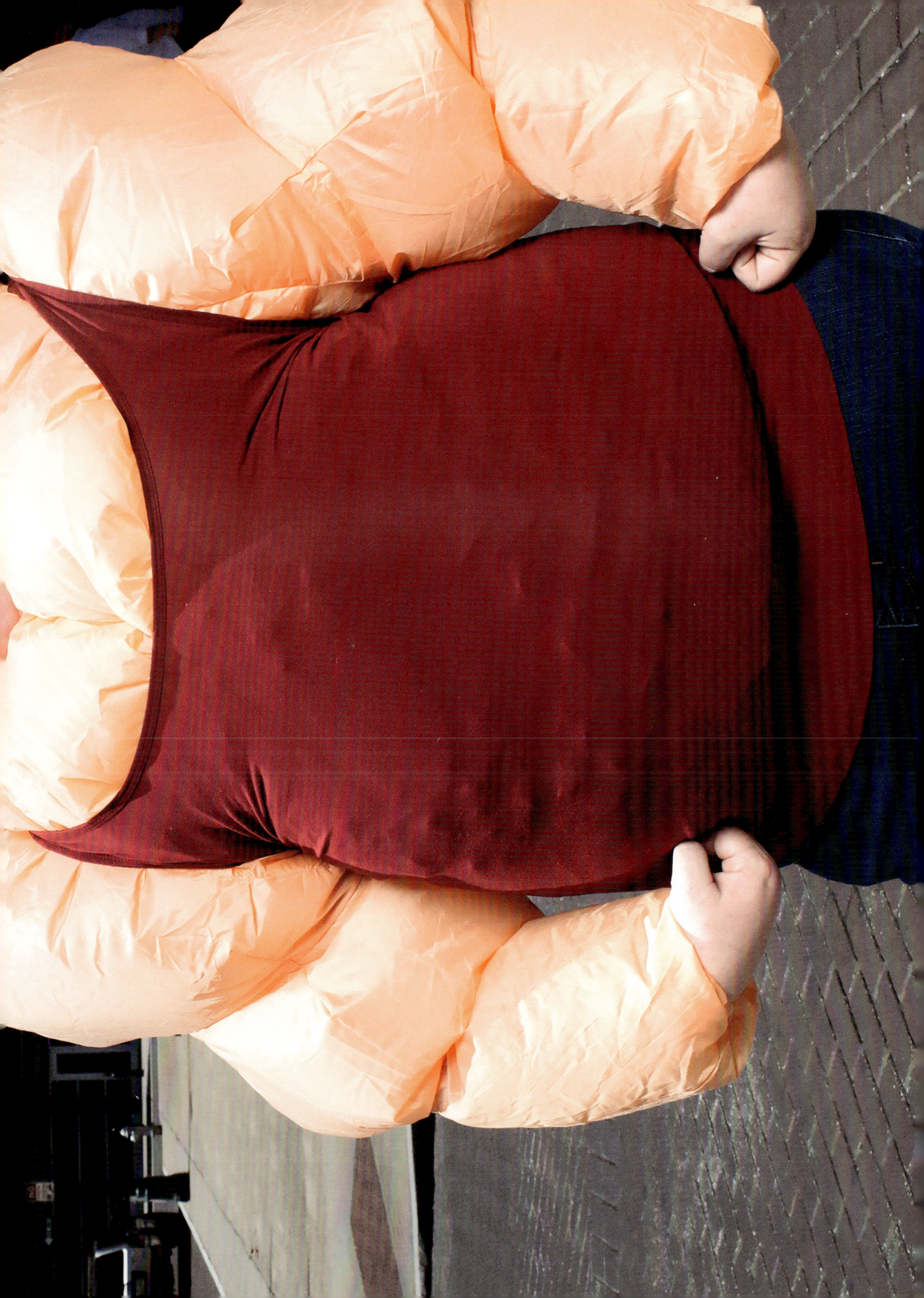

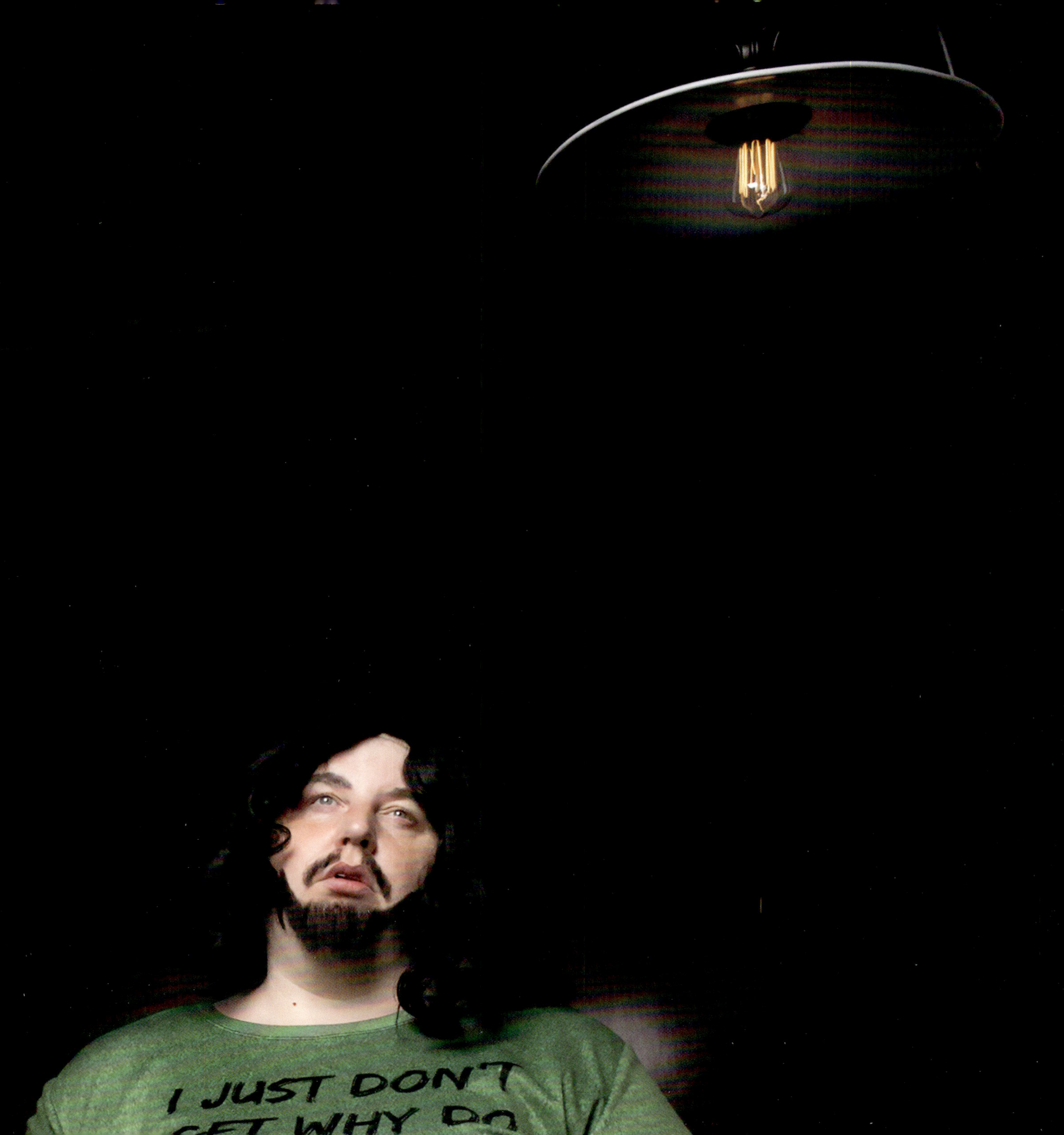
I JUST DON'T
GET WHY DO

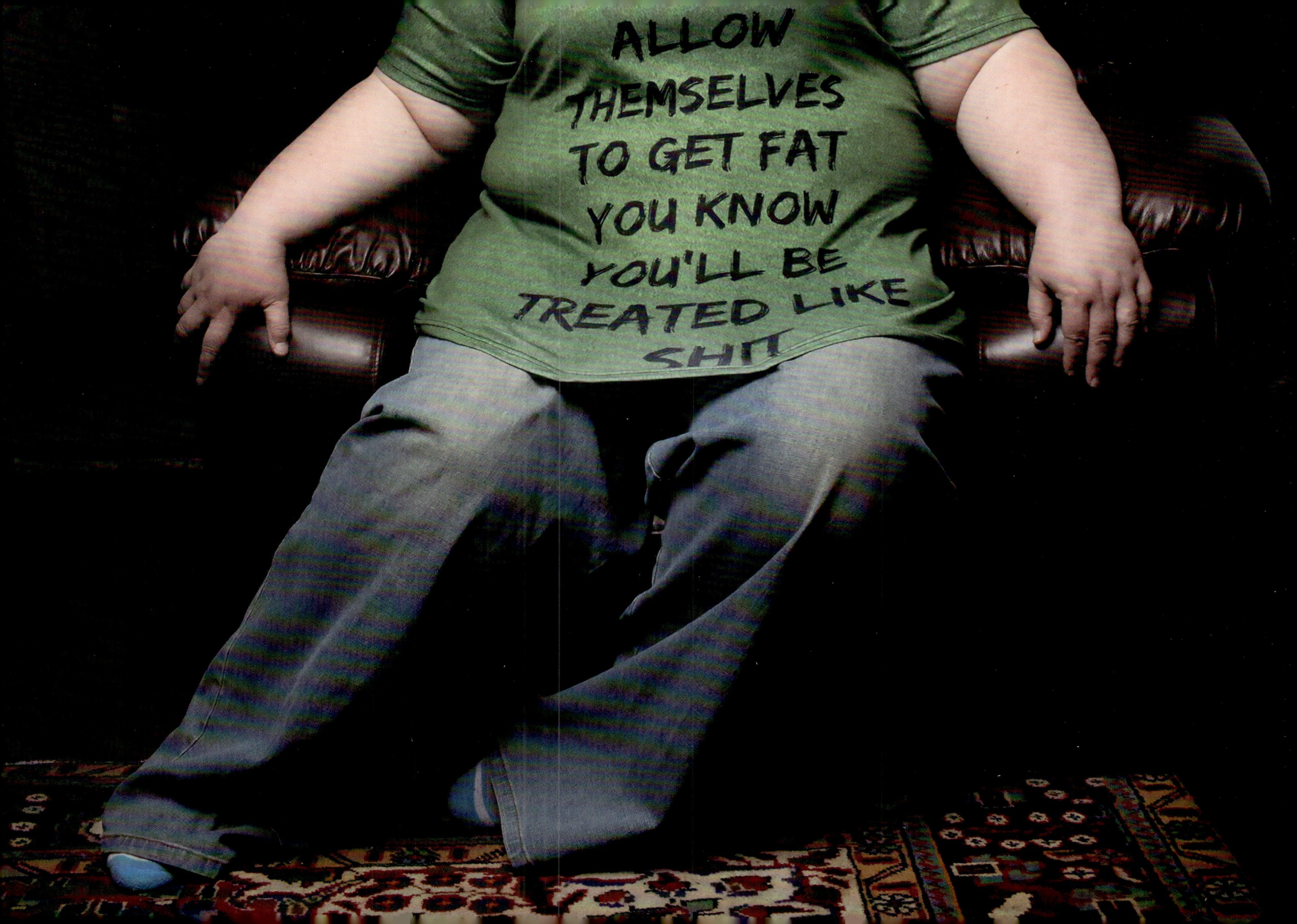

ALLOW
THEMSELVES
TO GET FAT
YOU KNOW
YOU'LL BE
TREATED LIKE
SHIT

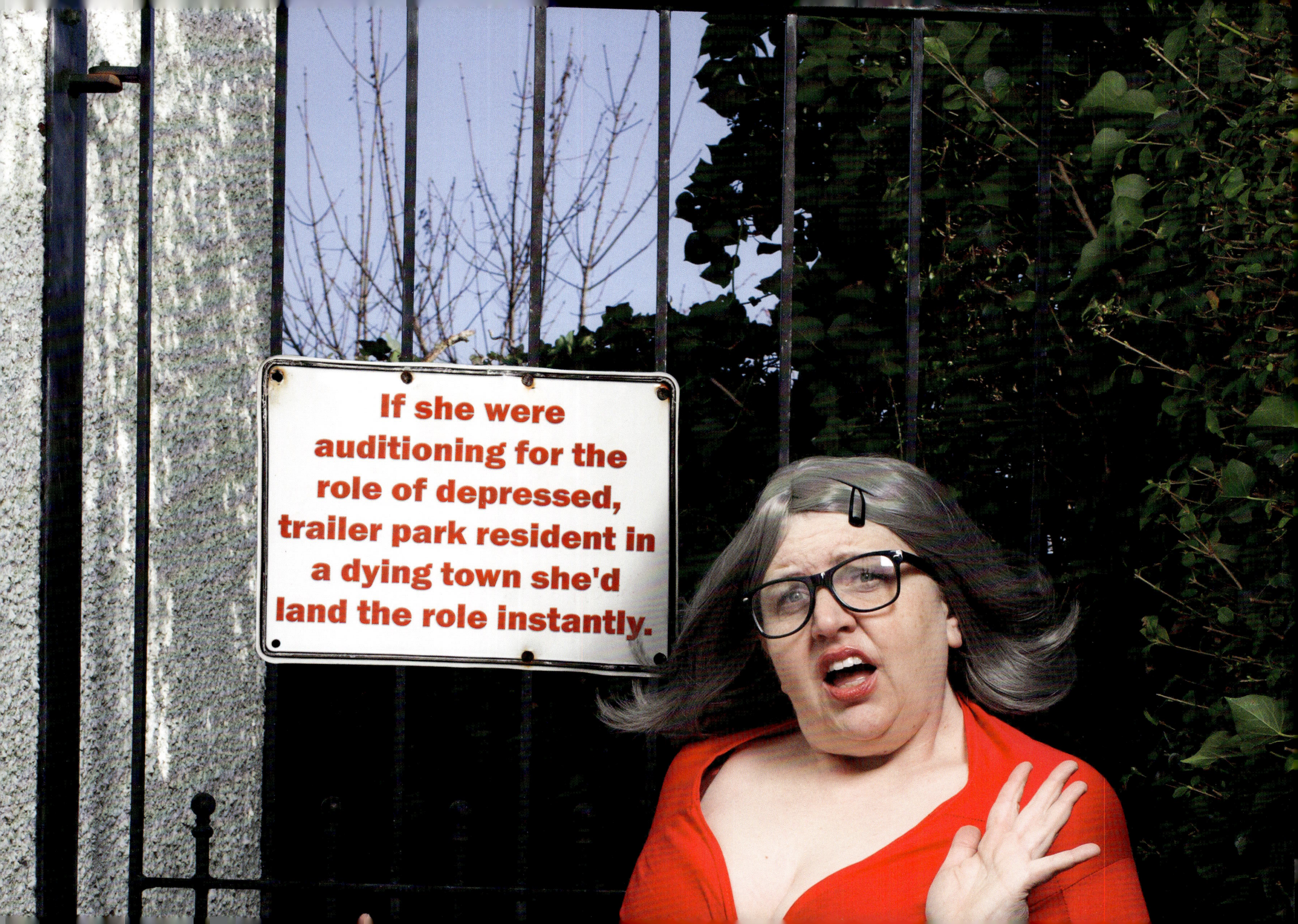
If she were
auditioning for the
role of depressed,
trailer park resident in
a dying town she'd
land the role instantly.

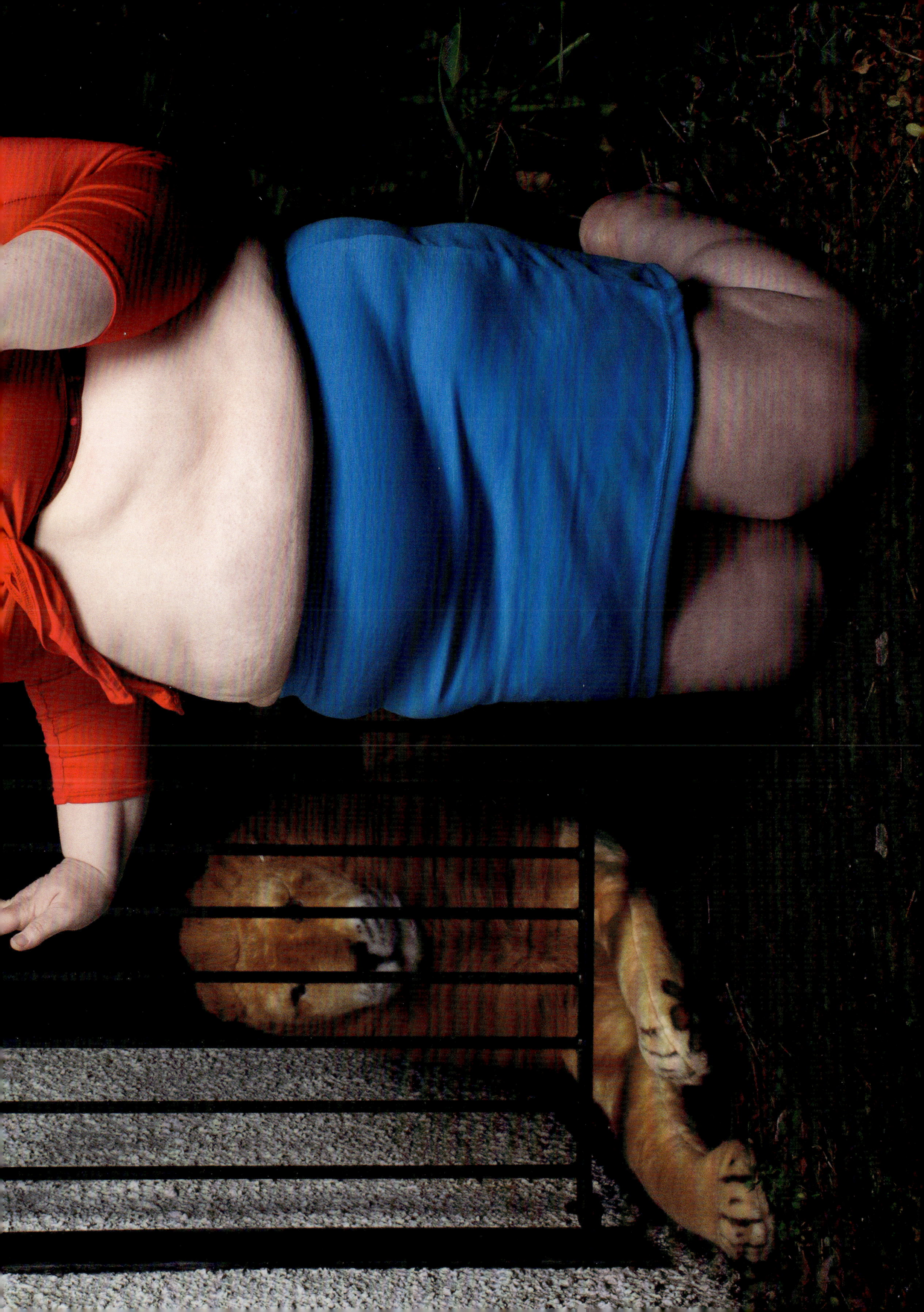

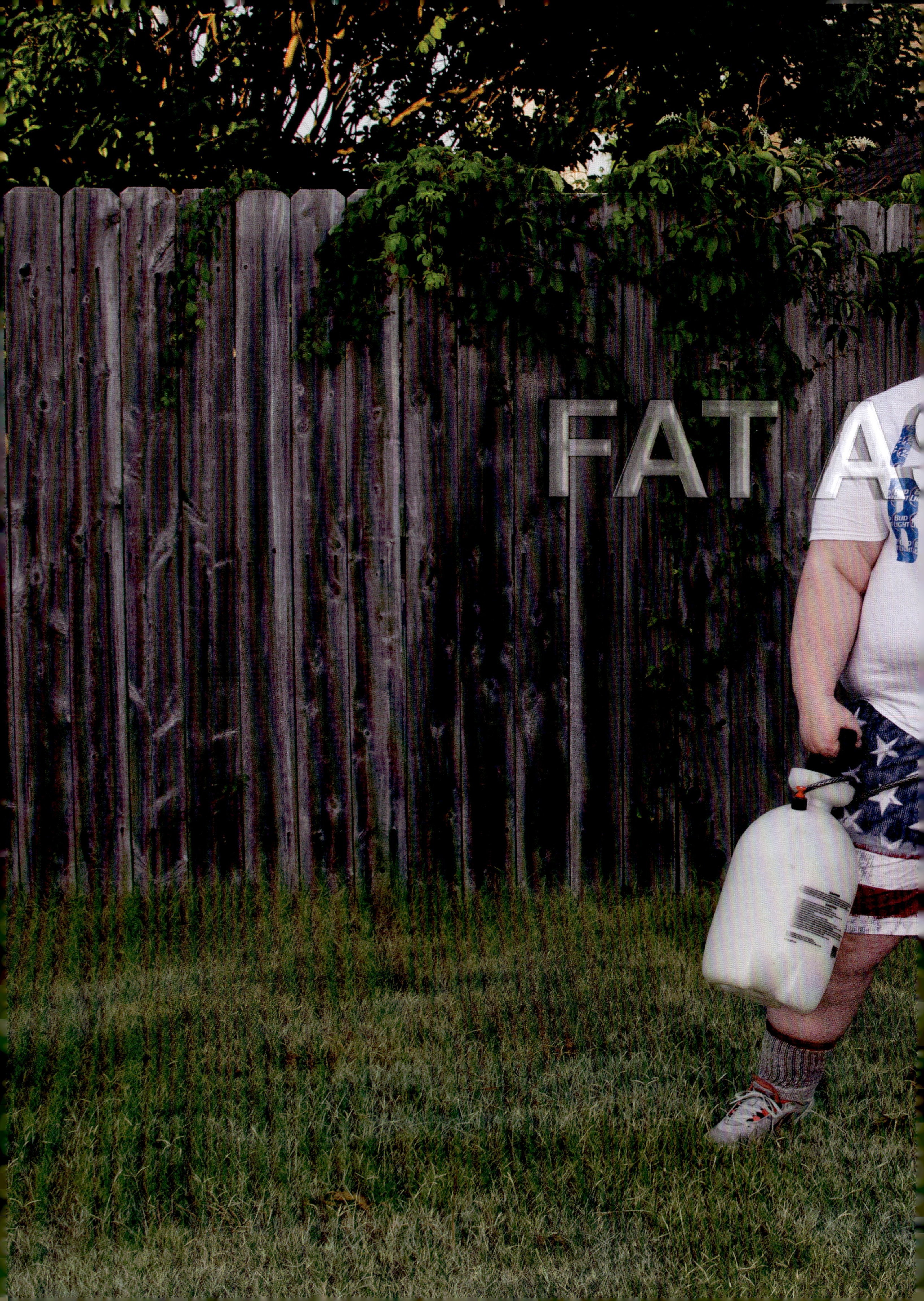

FAT A

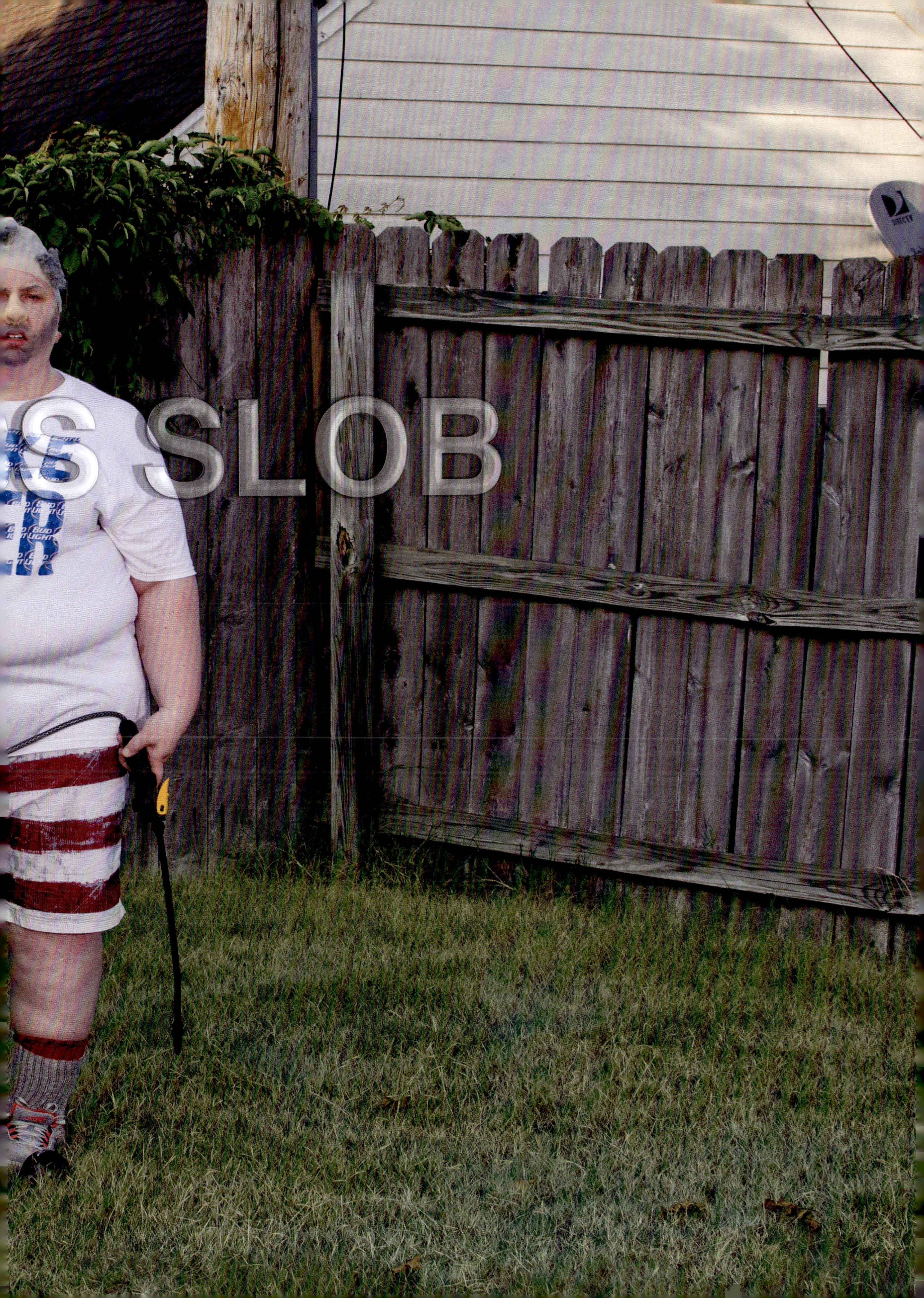
SLOB

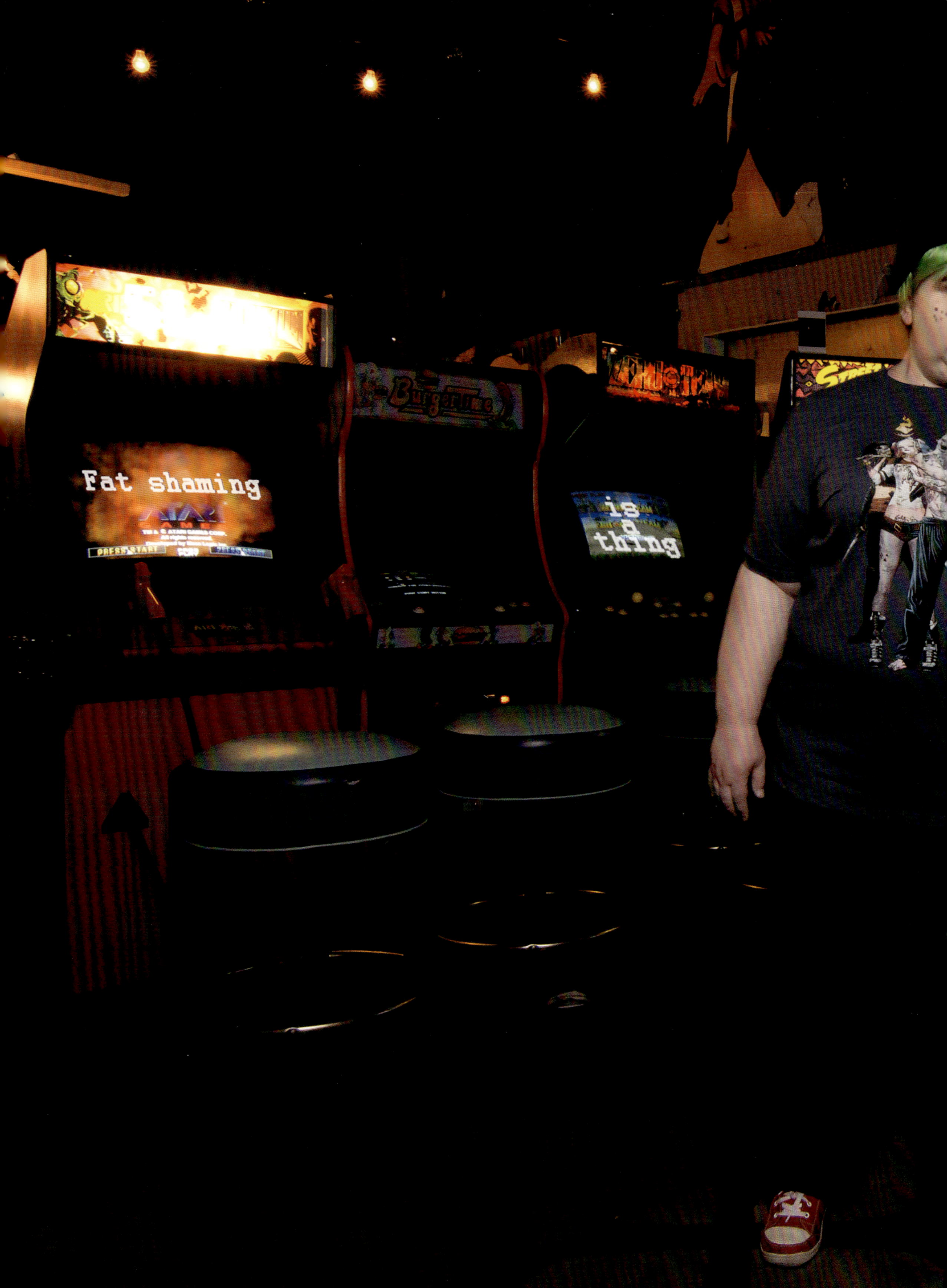

Fat shaming
is a thing

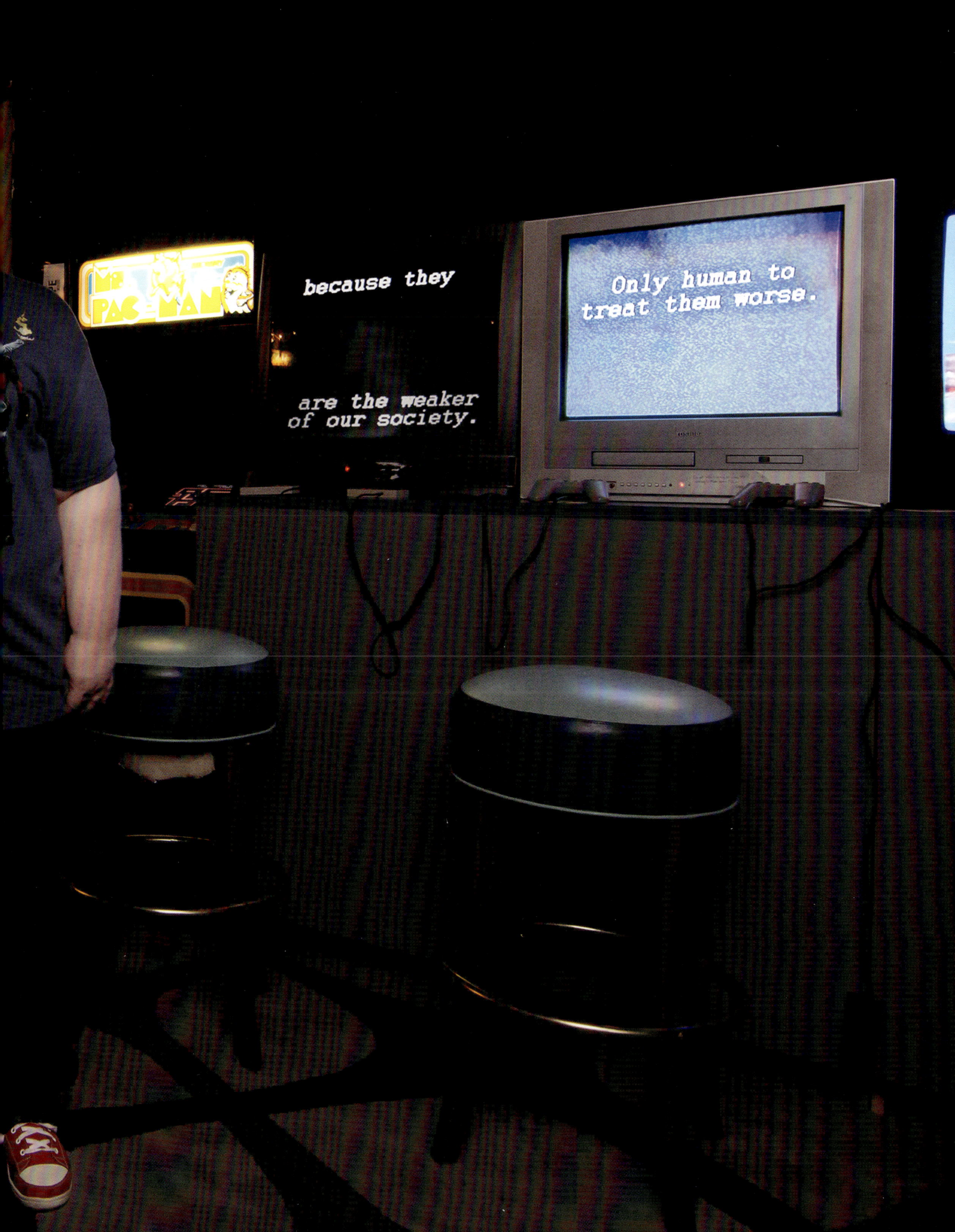
Ms PAC-MAN
because they
are the weaker
of our society.
Only human to
treat them worse.

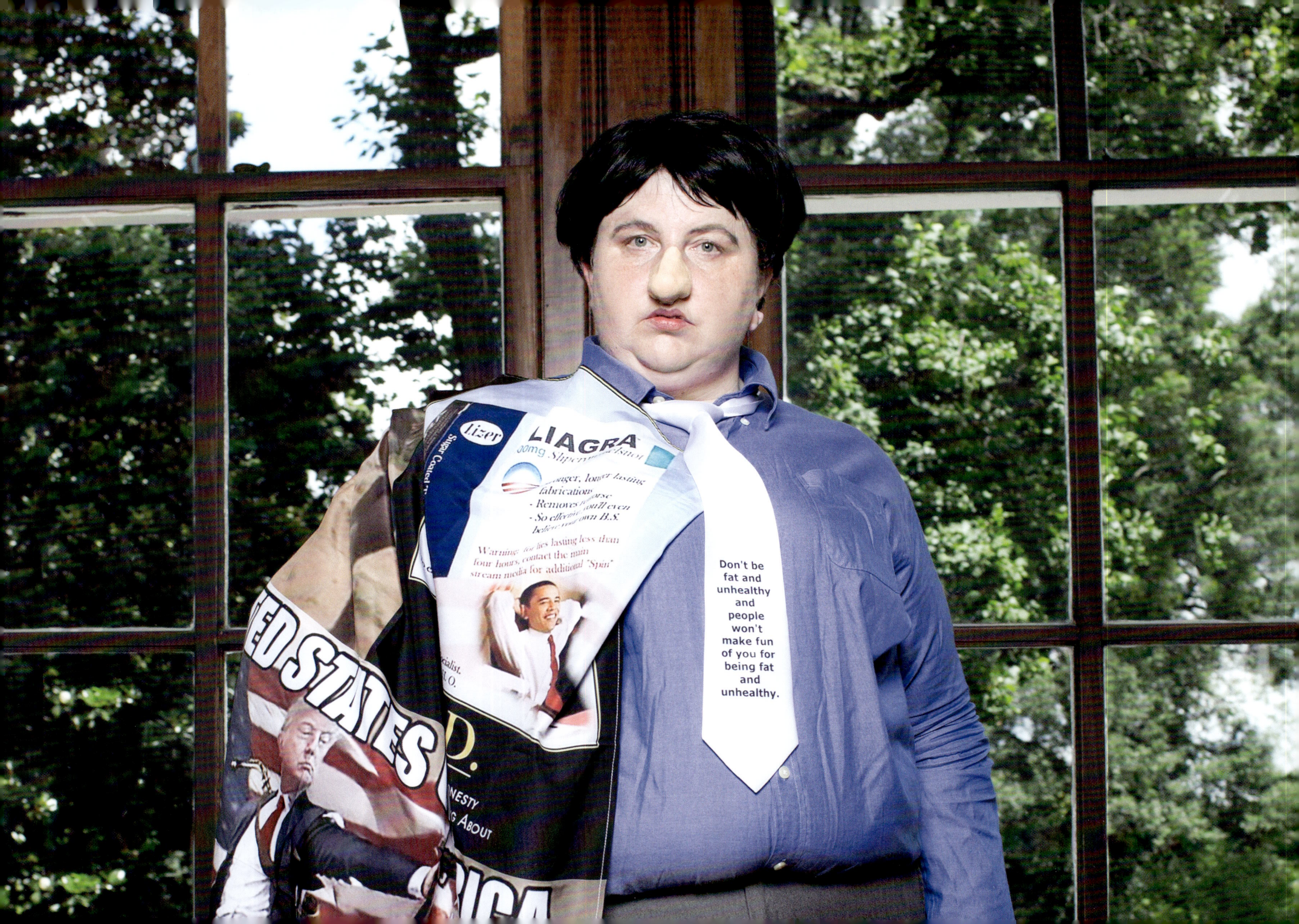

Lizer
Sugar Coated
LIAGRA
00mg Slip-every-ection
stronger, longer lasting fabrication
- Removes remorse
- So effective you'll even believe your own B.S.
Warning: for lies lasting less than four hours, contact the main stream media for additional "Spin"
Don't be fat and unhealthy and people won't make fun of you for being fat and unhealthy.
UNITED STATES

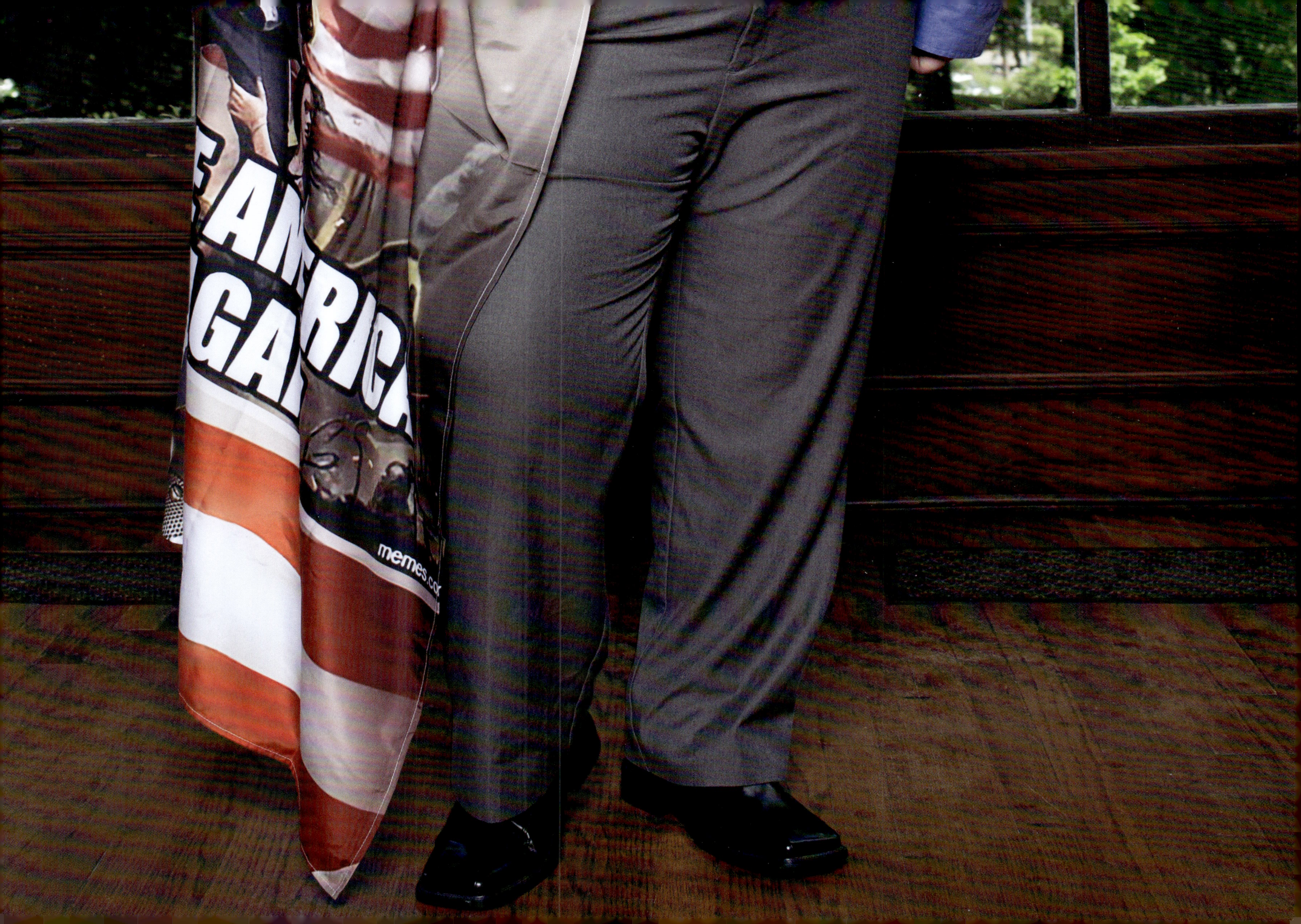
AMERIC
GA
memes.co

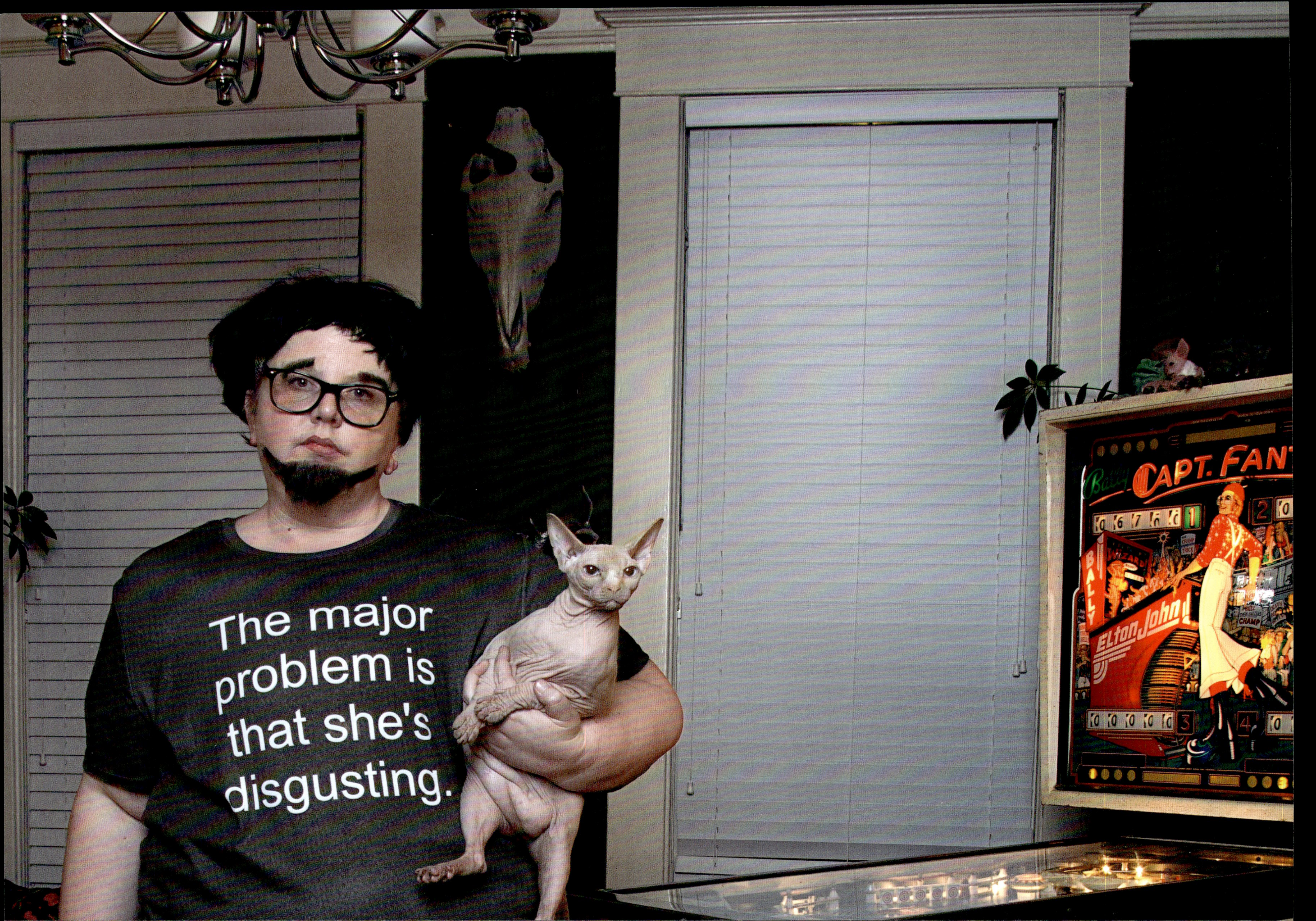
The major problem is that she's disgusting.

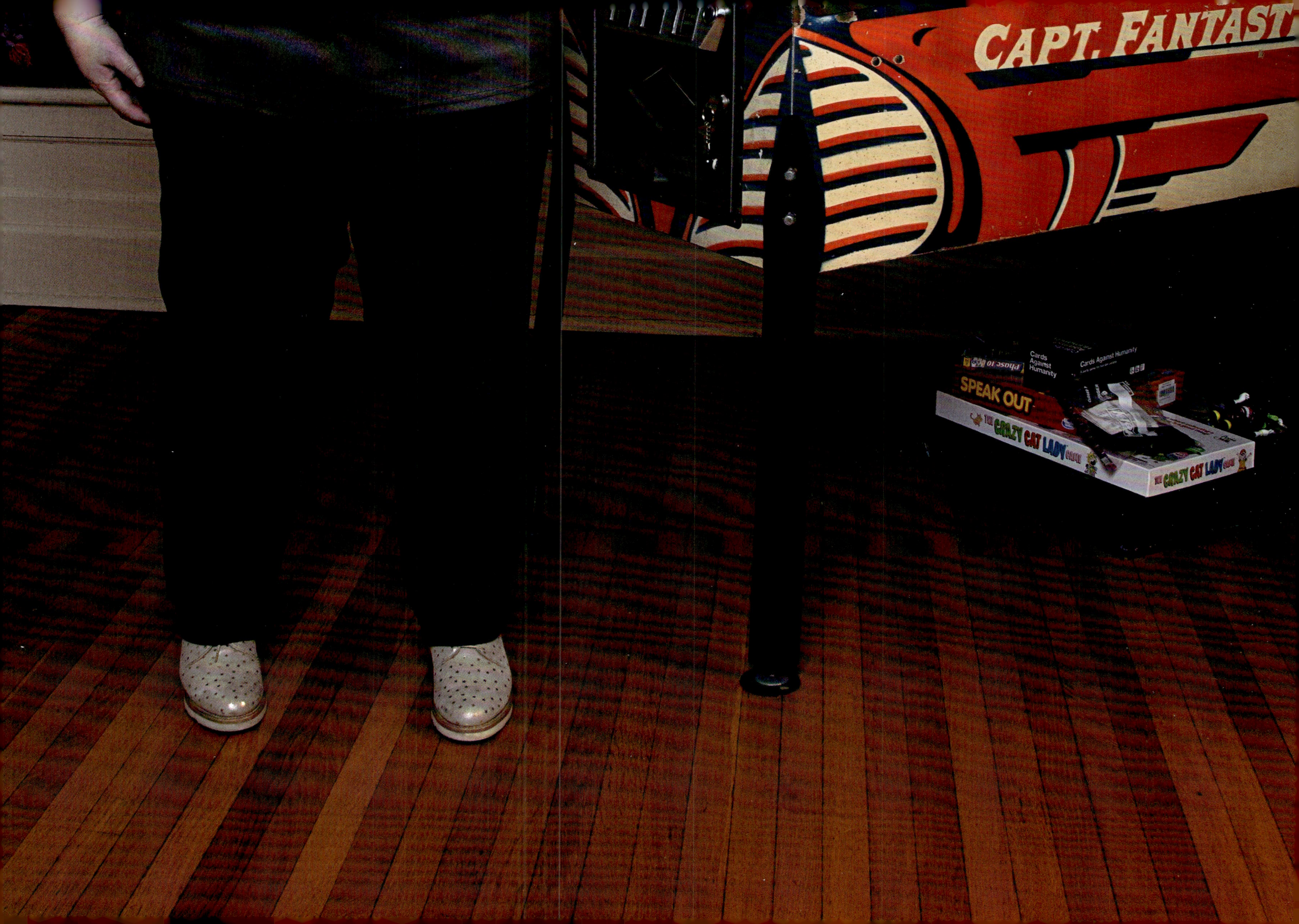

CAPT. FANTASTIC
Cards Against Humanity
Cards Against Humanity
Phase 10
SPEAK OUT
THE CRAZY CAT LADY GAME
THE CRAZY CAT LADY GAME

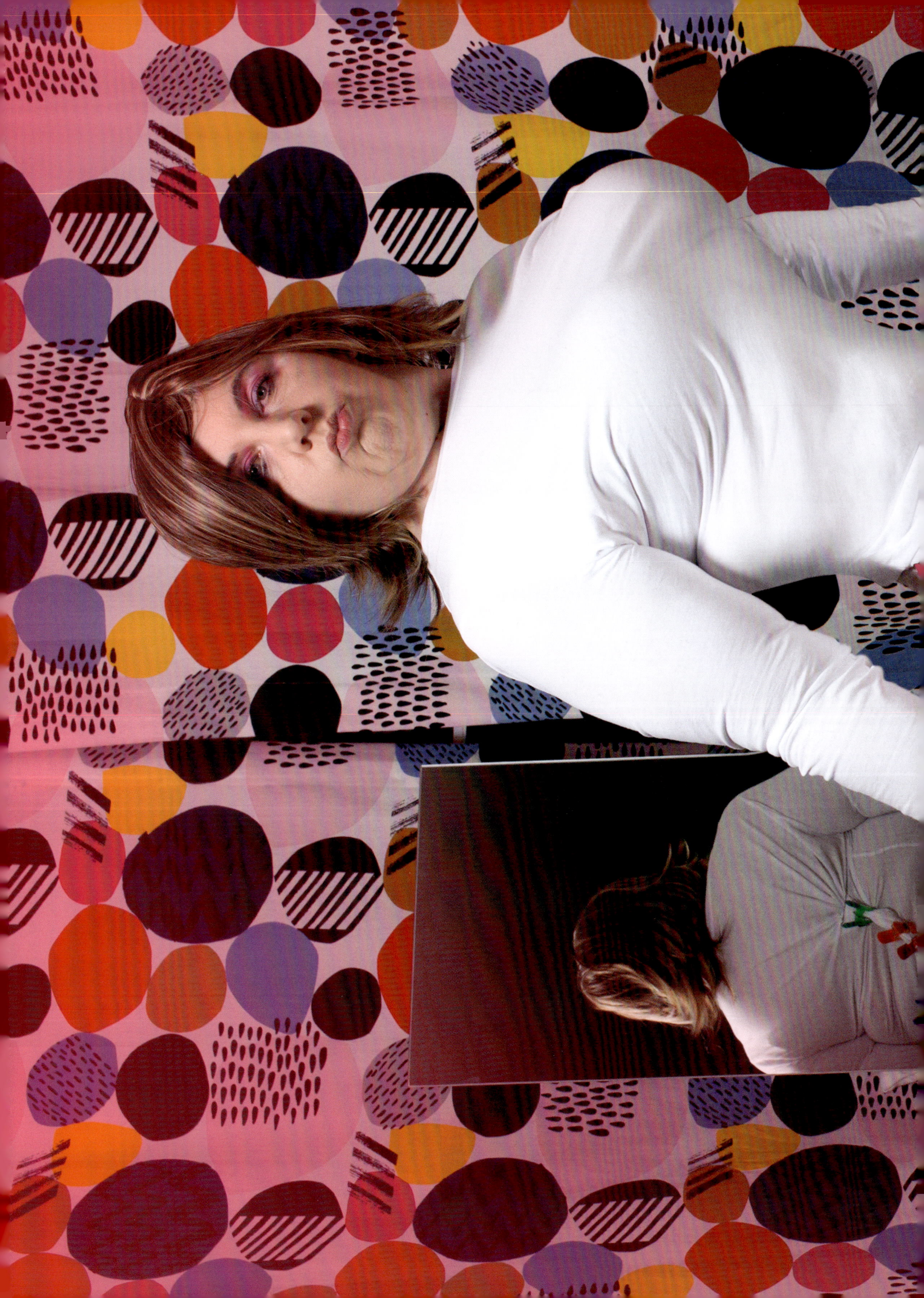

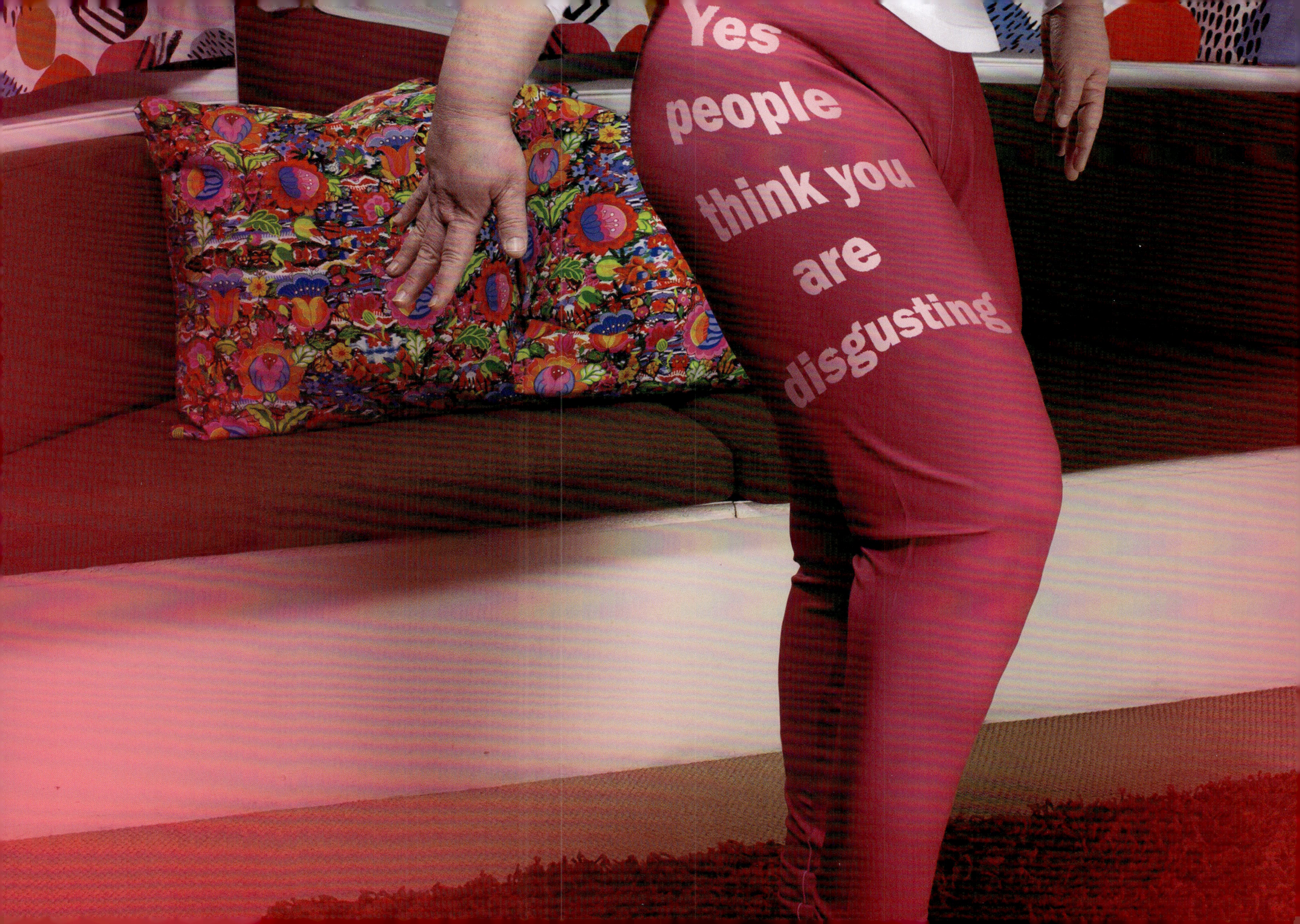

Yes
people
think you
are
disgusting

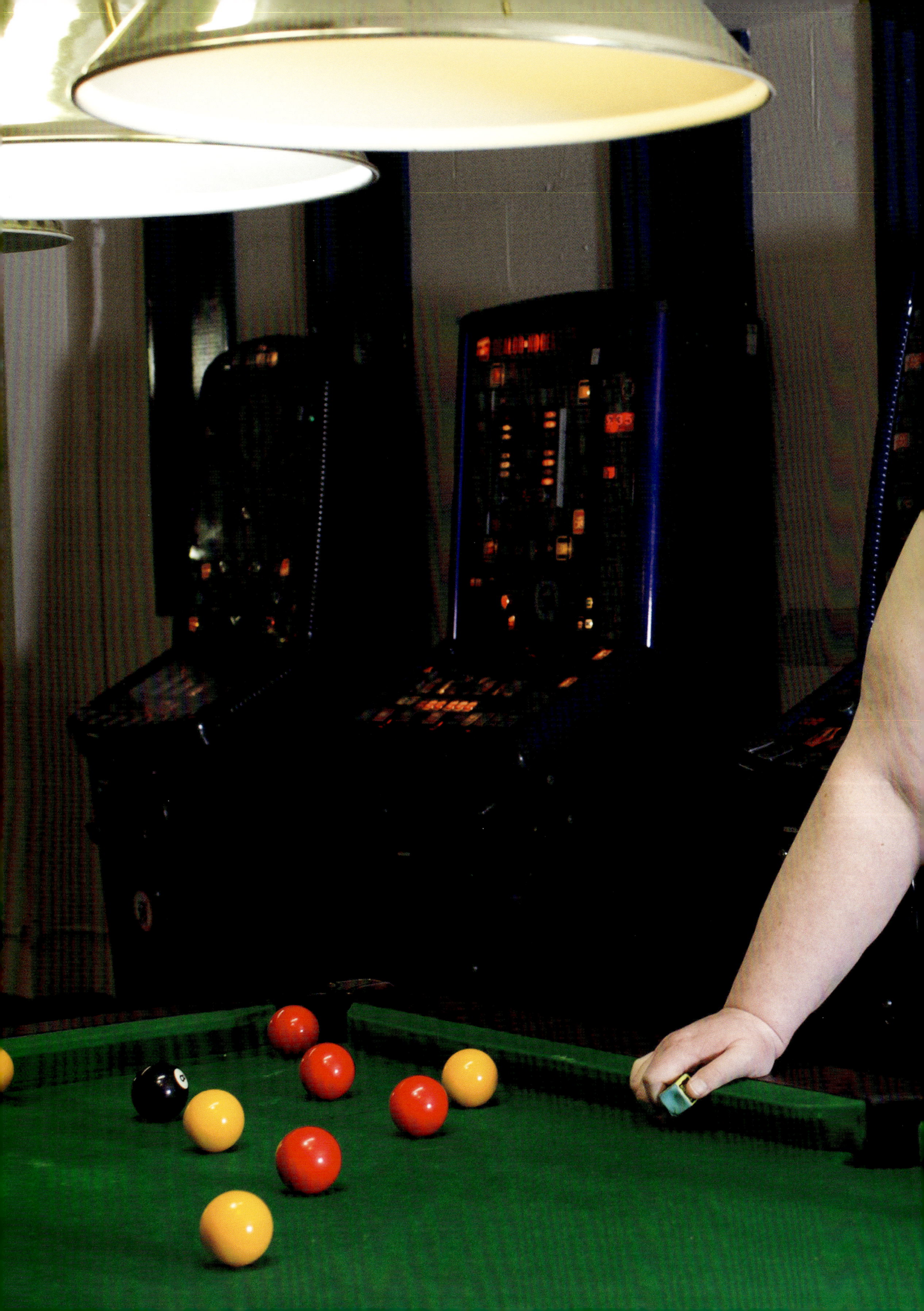

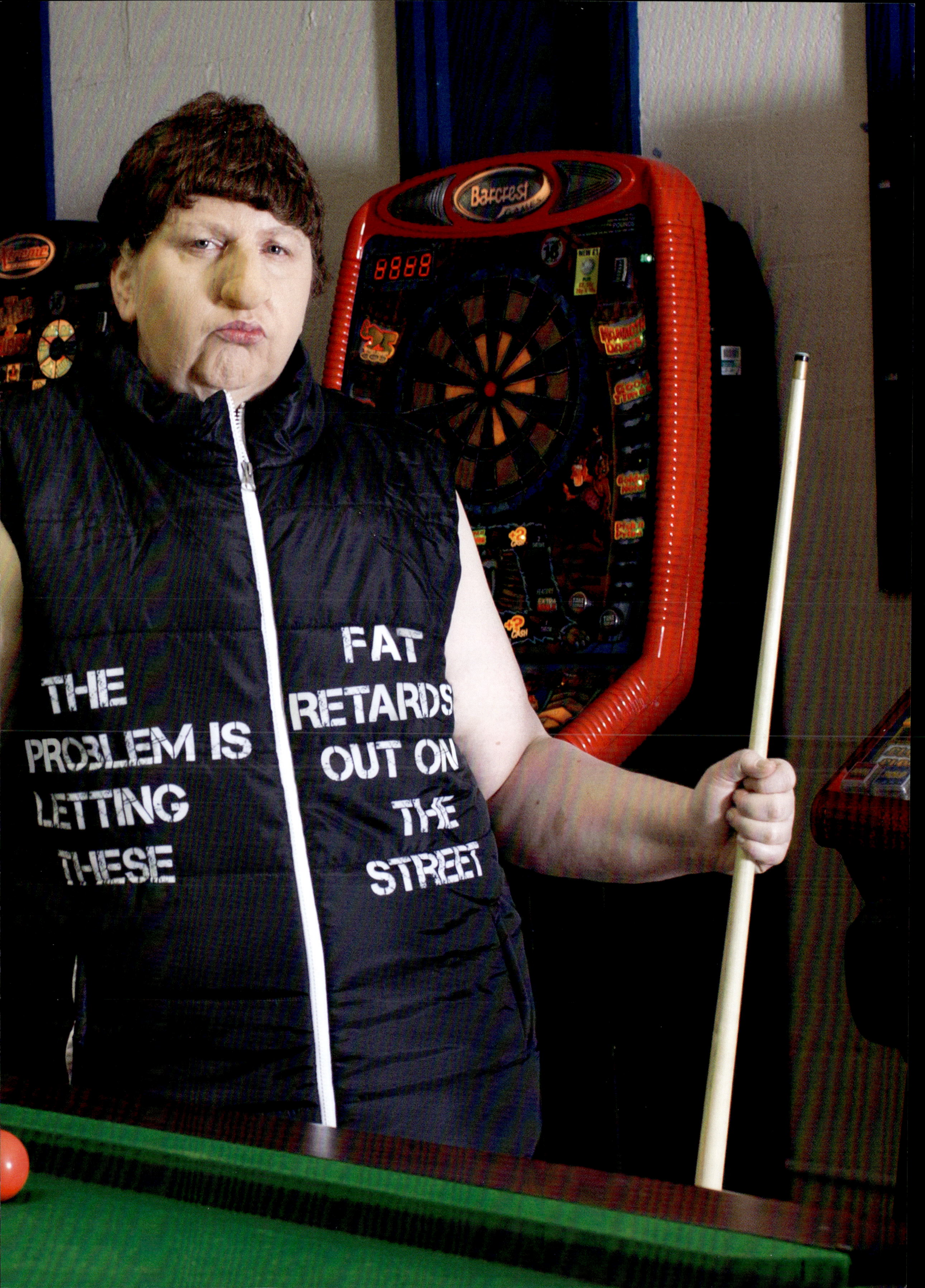

THE
PROBLEM IS
LETTING
THESE
FAT
RETARDS
OUT ON
THE
STREET
Barcrest

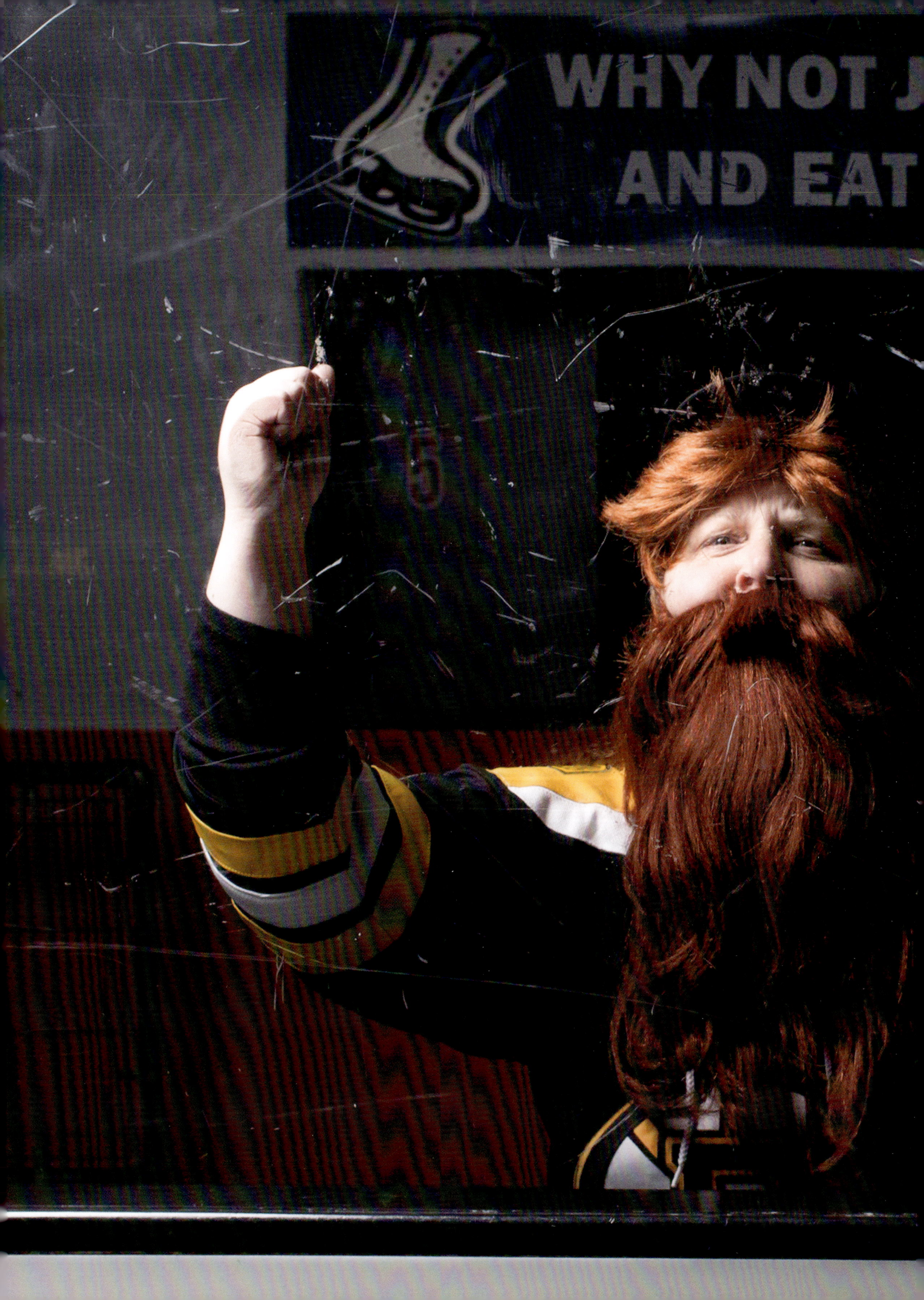

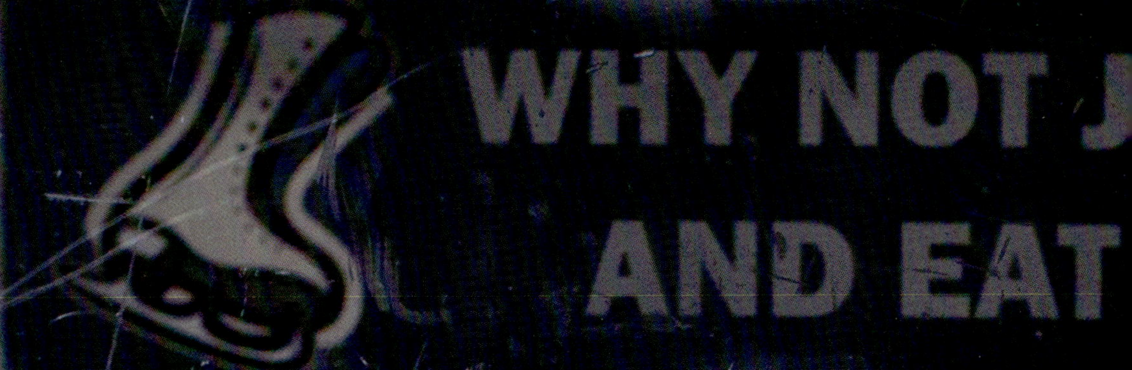

WHY NOT J
AND EAT

ST GO TO THE GYM
LITTLE BETTER?

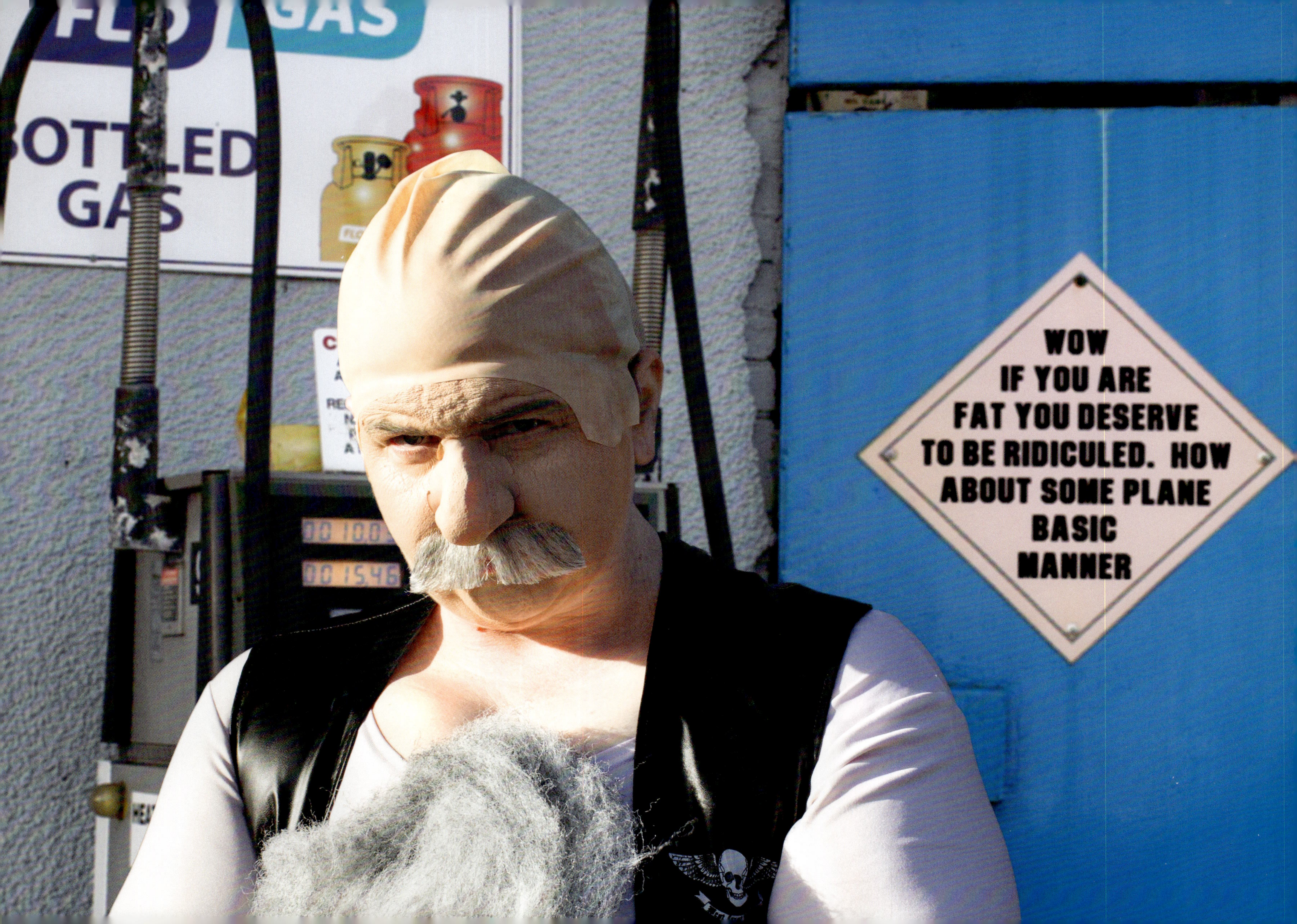

FLO GAS
BOTTLED GAS
WOW
IF YOU ARE
FAT YOU DESERVE
TO BE RIDICULED. HOW
ABOUT SOME PLANE
BASIC
MANNER

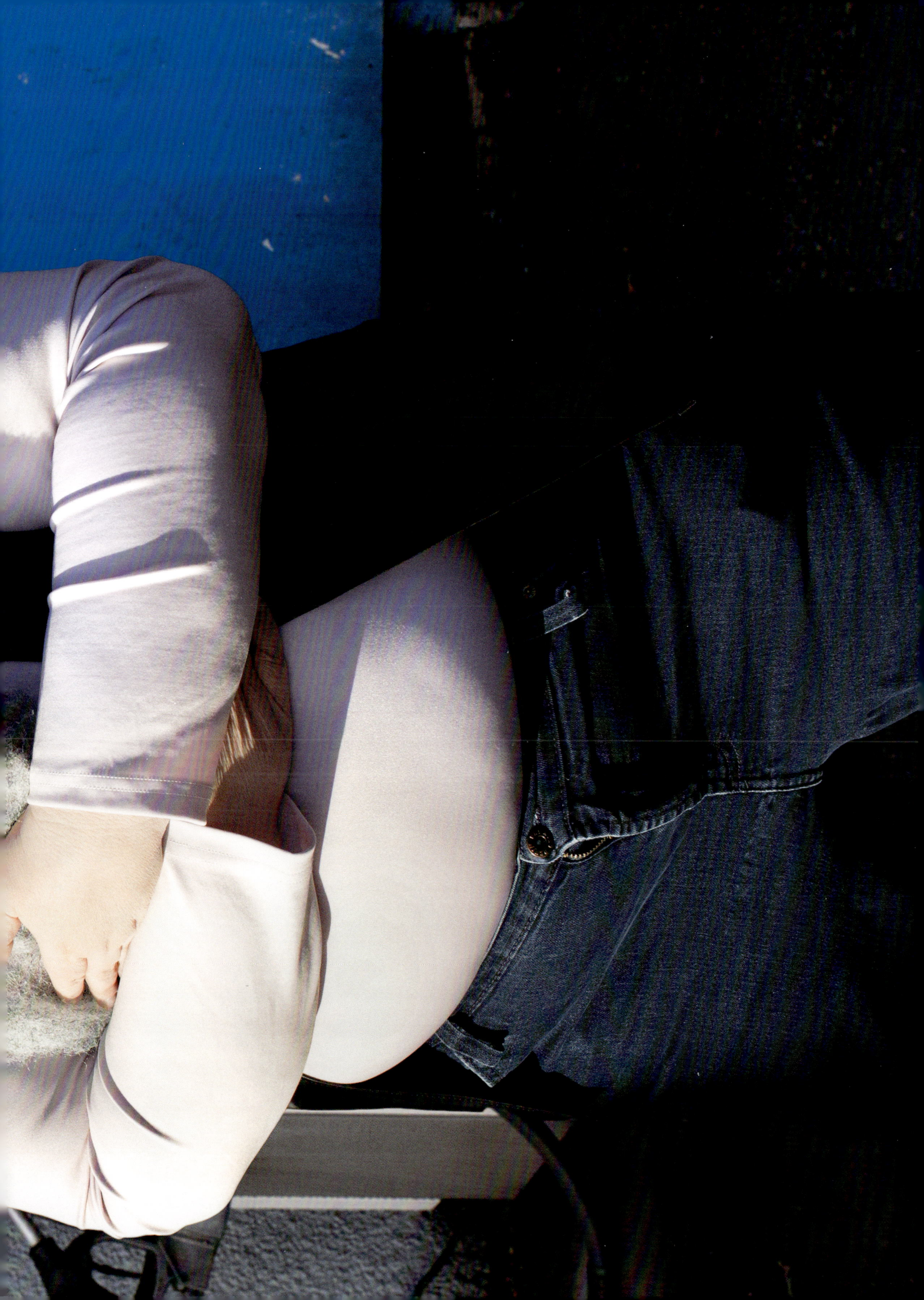

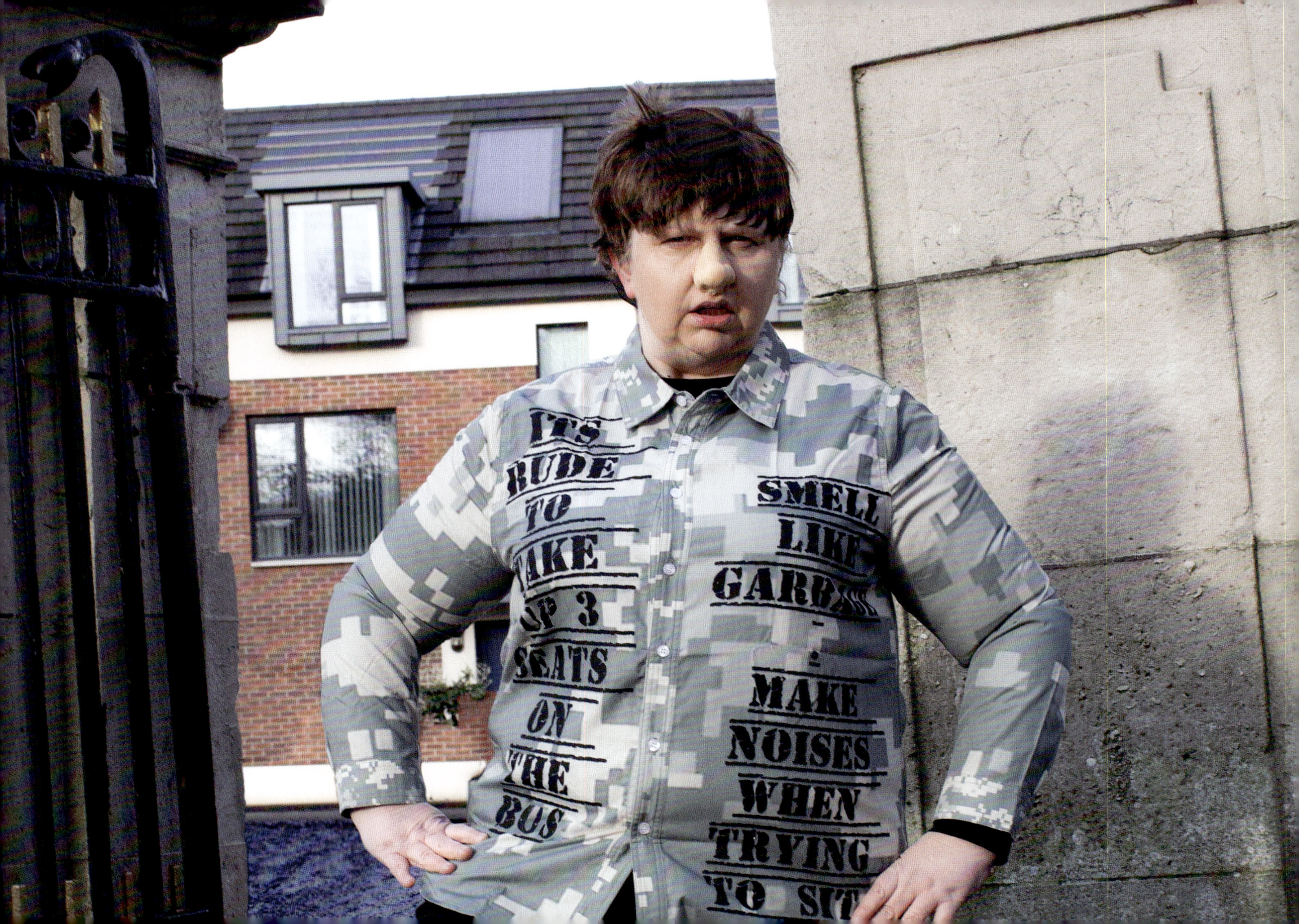
IT'S RUDE TO TAKE UP 3 SEATS ON THE BUS
SMELL LIKE GARBAGE
MAKE NOISES WHEN TRYING TO SIT

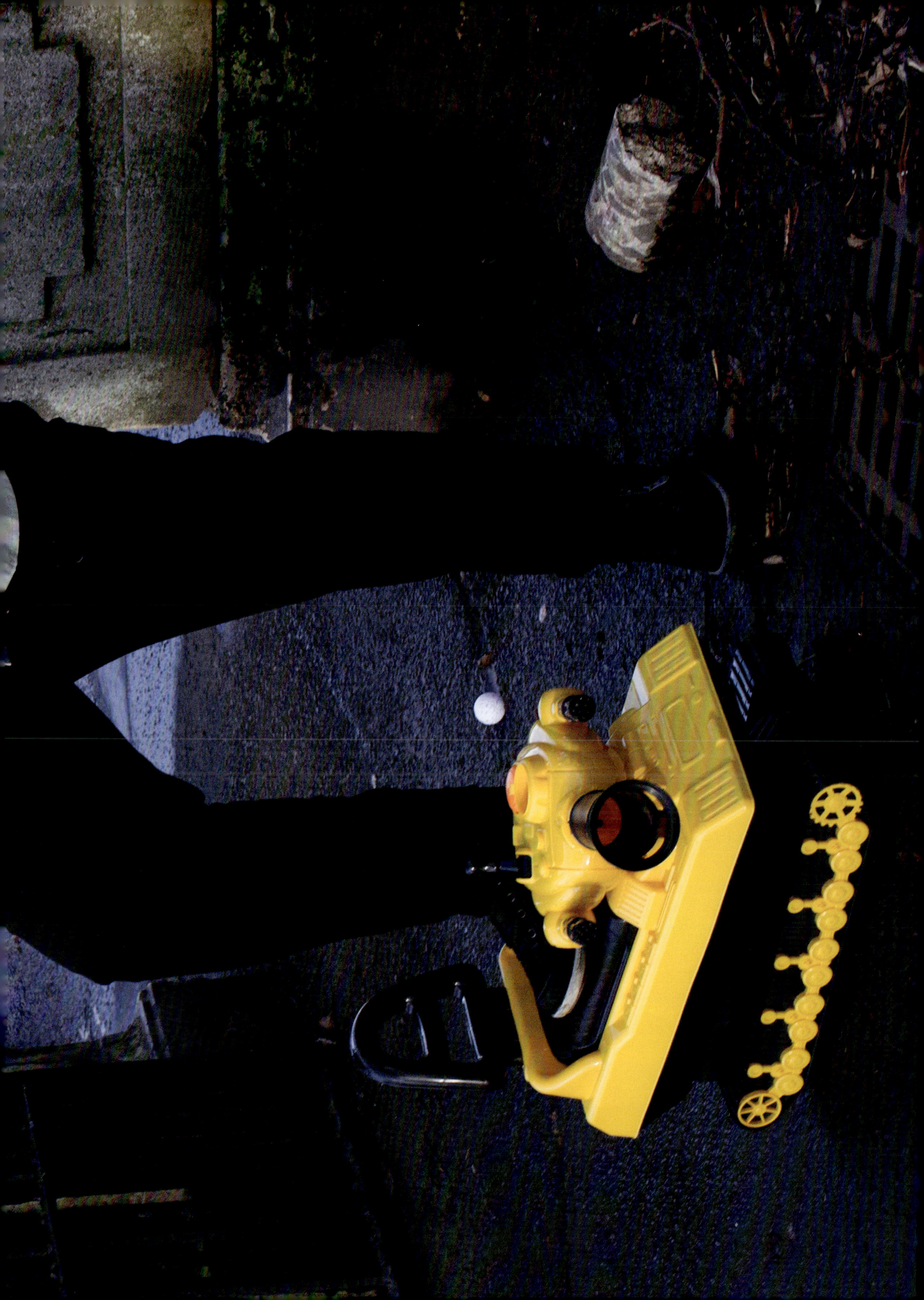

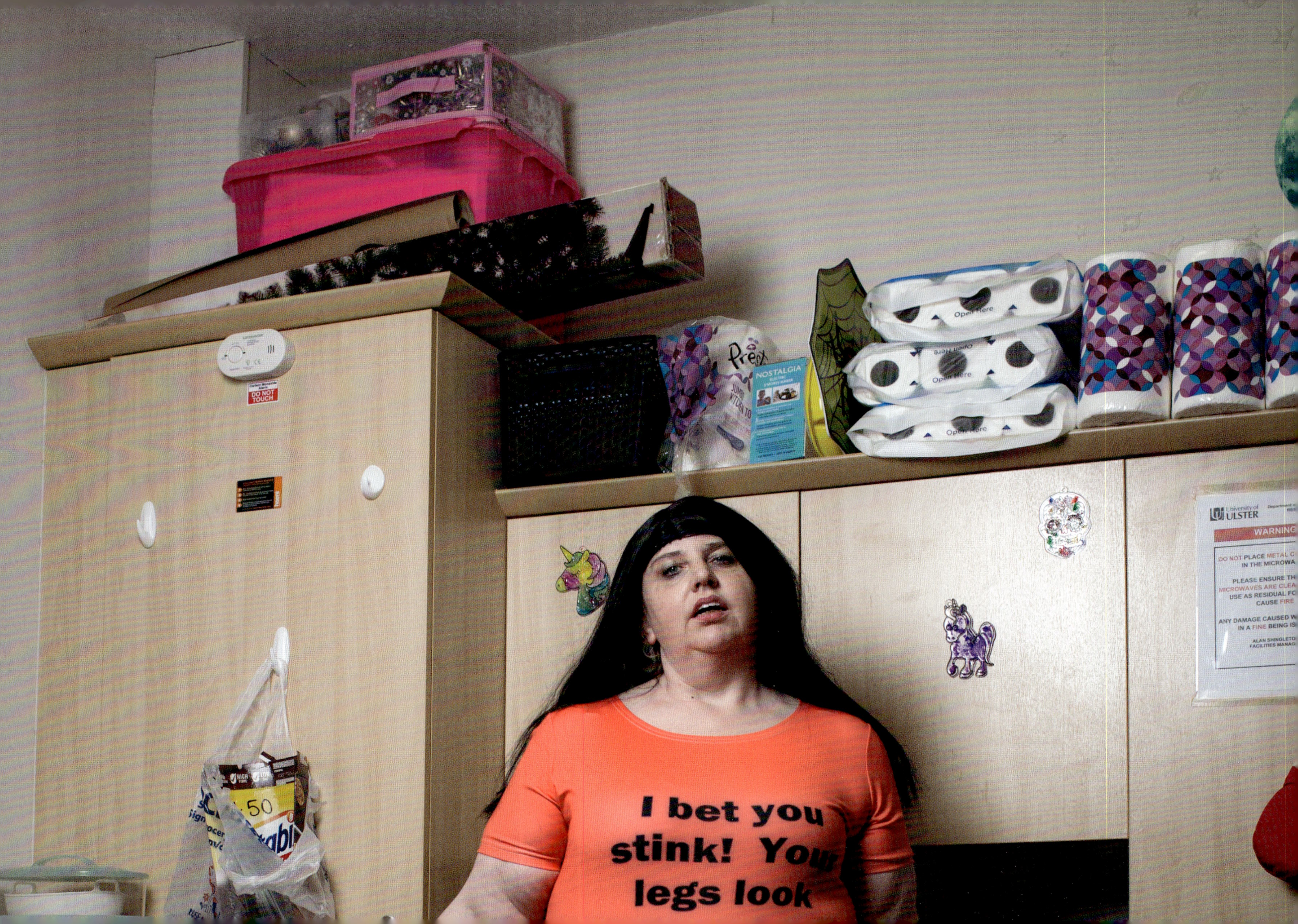

University of ULSTER
WARNING
DO NOT PLACE METAL C... IN THE MICROWA...
PLEASE ENSURE THE... MICROWAVES ARE CLEA... USE AS RESIDUAL FO... CAUSE FIRE
ANY DAMAGE CAUSED W... IN A FINE BEING IS...
ALAN SHINGLETO... FACILITIES MANAG...

I bet you stink! Your legs look

NOSTALGIA
Prex
Open Here
DO NOT TOUCH
.50

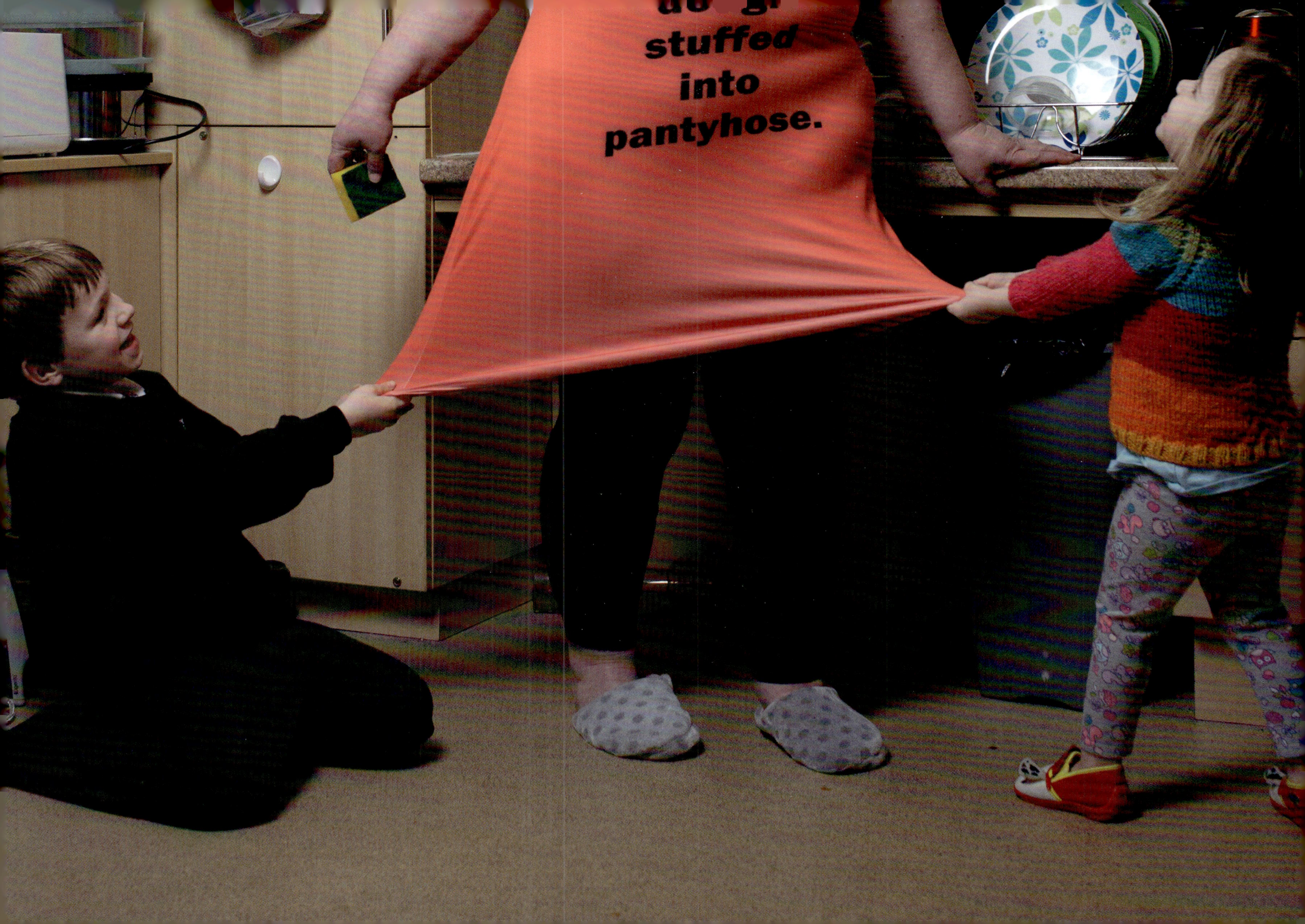

stuffed
into
pantyhose.

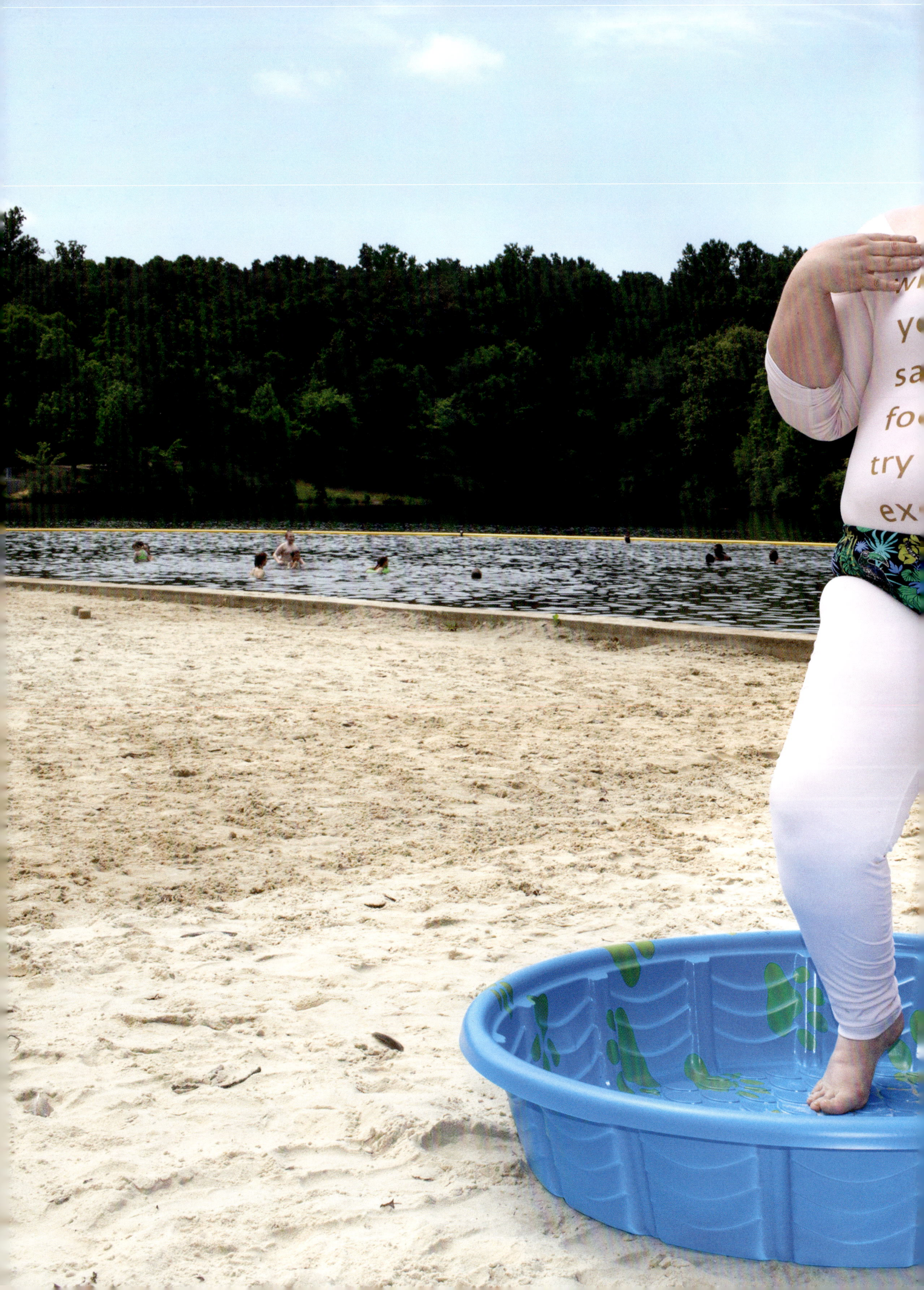

y
sa
fo
try
ex

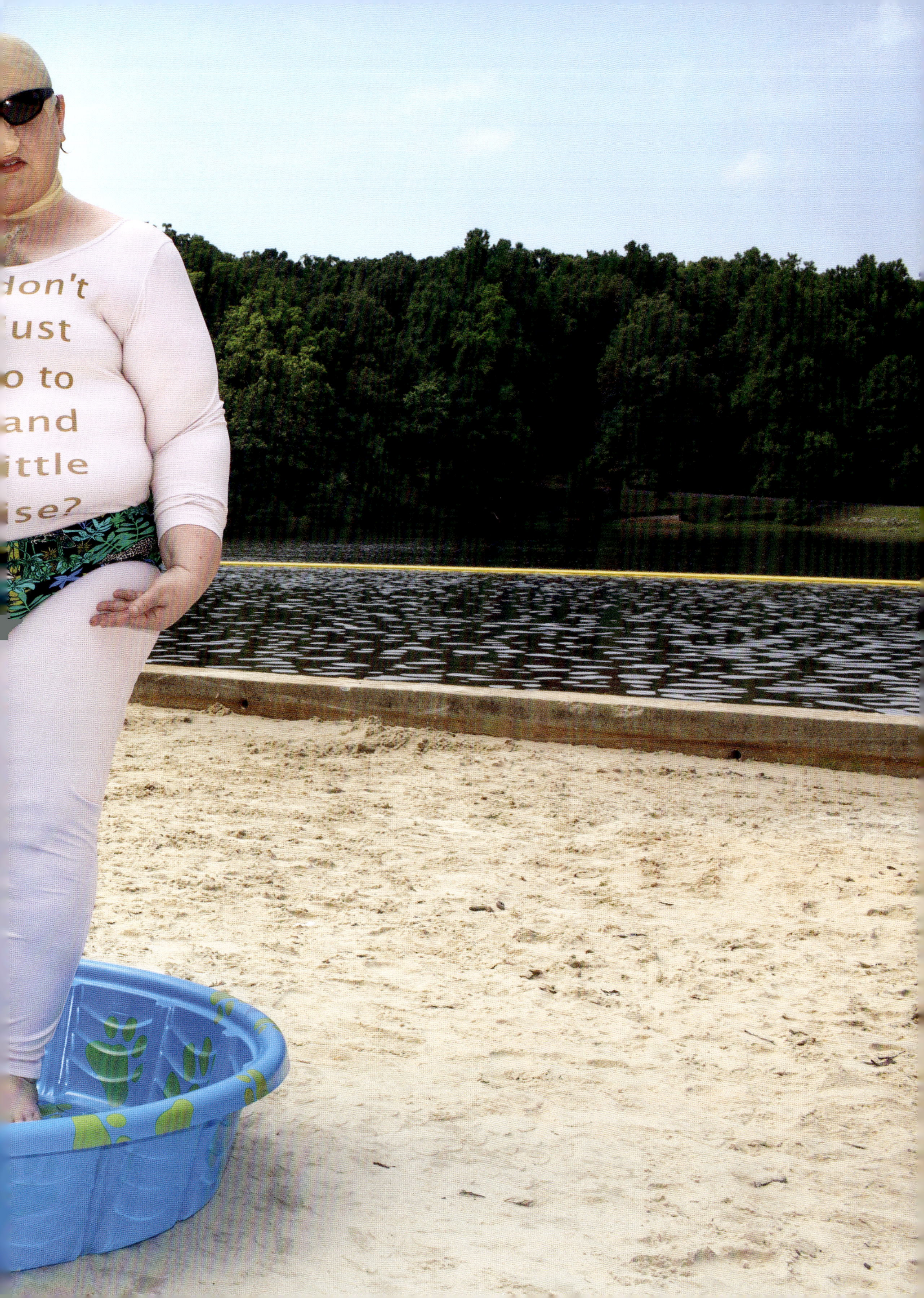
don't
ust
o to
and
ittle
se?

Titles —

On Bullies and Burlesque
— Emma Lewis, February 2019

Haley Morris-Cafiero can tell you the date in 2013 that Pope Benedict XVI resigned, because that's when her phone stopped ringing. For weeks until this point, journalists had been contacting her around the clock to request comments and soundbites on her series Wait Watchers. In this photography project-cum-social experiment, Morris-Cafiero set up her camera in public places to capture ways in which passersby looked at her—from sideways glances to outright points and stares. The project had received coverage here and there since she began it in 2010, but when it was picked up by Huffpost three years later, it went viral in a matter of hours.

Incubated in the murky cavities that online communities can become, negativity about Morris-Cafiero spread indiscriminately across social media, content forums, and blogs. Some remarks appeared to be for the benefit of fellow commenters: jokes or declaratives typed out with a metaphorical hand-to-mouth and snicker. Others addressed her directly. More surprising, a few felt compelled to email Morris-Cafiero lengthy diatribes spelling out exactly what they thought of her. Fat. Ugly. An embarrassment to her profession. An embarrassment to herself. The first time a message like this landed in Morris-Cafiero's inbox, she laughed

For the next few years, Morris-Cafiero collected this 'feedback': screengrab after screengrab until she was 1,000 images deep in inherently cowardly, depressingly 21st-century expressions of vitriol. Among the things that struck her was the ways in which people shape-shift online: 'virtue signaling' to friends and followers; spitting out bile in places those same people likely won't see. Just as it was clear that these cyberbullies don't care for actual dialogue with Morris-Cafiero, it was also clear these spaces made them feel empowered. The online forum as their pulpit: a place that promised they would be seen and heard.

What Morris-Cafiero wanted these cyberbullies to hear, in turn, was that attention of this kind is not opt-in only. The internet has a long memory, and she wanted to hold them to account. 'I see you,' her images say, 'and guess what? You're not immune'.

It wasn't difficult for Morris-Cafiero to access the bullies' online profiles and their portraits, most often selfies, presumably chosen to convey their desirability, politics, or social status. It was easy enough, too, to find the clothes and props that would allow her to create successful parodies of these images. The inability to divorce their profile pictures from their words was crucial to the idea of accountability. So, across their clothing, in the place where slogans would usually appear, she plastered their comments to her in bold type—like branding of a different kind.

In many ways, The Bully Pulpit is a project about visibility: Morris-Cafiero's visibility on the street, her then visibility online, the desire of her bullies to be seen, and the act of her exposé. The technique of masquerade is a continuation of this idea: Morris-Cafiero literally throws these individuals into the spotlight their images suggest they desire, but at the same time her costumes are deliberately absurd, her prosthetics intentionally crude. It's classic burlesque. Probably the most infuriating thing of all for her bullies is that she looks like she's having a really good time.

Bio —

Part performer, part artist, part provocateur, part spectator, Haley Morris-Cafiero explores the act of reflection in her photography. Morris-Cafiero's photographs have been widely exhibited in solo and group exhibitions throughout the United States and abroad, and have been featured in numerous newspapers, magazines and online, including Le Monde, New York Magazine, and Salon. Born in Atlanta, she is a graduate of the University of North Florida, where she earned a BA in Photography and a BFA in Ceramics in 1999. She holds a MFA from the University of Arizona in Art. Nominated for the Prix Pictet in 2014 and a 2016 Fulbright finalist, The Magenta Foundation published her monograph, The Watchers, in 2015. Morris-Cafiero moved to Belfast in the fall of 2018 to teach photography at the Belfast School of Art at Ulster University.

Thank you —

I couldn't have done this project without the support of people who helped me move equipment, stand in the cold and the wind, and roll around with whales: Ryan Steed, Suzie Hansen, Abbey Bratcher, and Ben Malcolmson. Dustin Lester is the hero of all postproduction heroes. I thank Charles Guice for believing in me and giving vital feedback throughout the project, Emma Lewis for her wonderful writing and great conversations about the project, Hannah Watson, TJ Boulting Gallery for showing the work and being a true friend and advocate, and also Meghann Riepenhoff for her sage words. There are so many people who inspire and support me, but none of this would be possible without my Catch who will do anything to help me fulfill my dream.

This project was made possible by an ArtsAccelerator Grant funded by ArtsMemphis.

This monograph was supported by Ulster University, Belfast School of Art, Strategic Support for Research Fund.

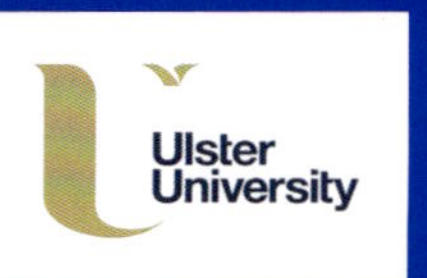

FALL
LINE

Fall Line Press
675 Drewry Street, Suite 6
Atlanta, Georgia 30306
www.falllinepress.com

Book Design: Margaux Fraisse
Photo Editors: William Boling & Clay Jordan
Copy Editor: Megan Sexton

First Edition

Printed and bound by SYL, Barcelona

Library of Congress Number 2019902988
ISBN 978-0-9986490-8-5

Website: haleymorriscafiero.com
Instagram: @hmorriscafiero

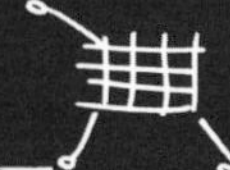

Fall Line Press would like to
acknowledge and thank TJ
Boulting Gallery and Trolley Books
of London for their collaboration
in distributing and supporting
The Bully Pulpitin the UK and EU.